Psychoanalysis in Focus

Counselling & Psychotherapy in Focus

Series Editor: Windy Dryden, Goldsmiths College,
University of London

Counselling & Psychotherapy in Focus is a series of books which
examines the criticisms directed at different forms of counselling
and psychotherapy. Each book in the series reviews the critiques of
a particular approach, presents counter-arguments to the criticisms
and examines the influence that the debates have had in shaping
the approach in question. The books in this series are:

Psychoanalysis in Focus
David Livingstone Smith

Family Therapy in Focus
Mark Rivett & Eddy Street

Person-Centred Therapy in Focus
Paul Wilkins

Psychoanalysis in Focus

David Livingstone Smith

SAGE Publications
London • Thousand Oaks • New Delhi

SAGE Publications Ltd
6 Bonhill Street
London EC2A 4PU

SAGE Publications Inc
2455 Teller Road
Thousand Oaks, California 91320

SAGE Publications India Pvt Ltd
B-42, Panchsheel Enclave
Post Box 4109
New Delhi 110 017

British Library Cataloguing in Publication data

A catalogue record for this book is available
from the British Library

ISBN 0 7619 6193 3
ISBN 0 7619 6194 1 (pbk)

Library of Congress Control Number: 2002108291

Typeset by C&M Digitals (P) Ltd., Chennai, India
Printed in Great Britain by TJ International Ltd, Padstow, Cornwall

To my Jamaican family: Elaine, Winston,
Ann Marie and Paul.

Praise for the Book

Psychoanalysis in Focus provides an excellent introduction to the basic problems besetting psychoanalytic theory and practice. David Livingstone Smith's lucid survey of the major strands of the critical debate about psychoanalysis fills an important gap in the literature of a discipline not renowned for examining its own shortcomings at a fundamental level.

Allen Esterson, Author of Seductive Mirage:
An Exploration of the Work of Sigmund Freud

David Livingstone Smith's clearly reasoned iconoclastic account convincingly demonstrates the illusory, quasi-religious status of psychoanalysis unsupported as it currently is by any objective evidence to underwrite the vast bulk of its propositions. If it is to ask meaningful questions about the human mind and find ways to answer them, it will need to evolve into an interdisciplinary science and thereby create links with evolutionary biology, anthropology, cognitive psychology, neuroscience and linguistics.

Ann Casement, Analytical Psychologist;
Fellow of the Royal Anthropological Institute

No responsible practitioner or scholar of psychoanalysis and psychotherapy can ignore this intellectually outstanding and grittily honest book. David Livingstone Smith brings together many of the themes that he has done so much to place on the agenda of contemporary psychoanalysis: the philosophical and scientific standing of the discipline; the nuanced impact of developments in related research fields; the oft-neglected role of the analyst in terms of communication between analyst and patient. What impresses me is the way in which Smith functions both as an educator, helping the reader to understand the significance of the challenges psychoanalysis faces, and also as a major protagonist in the debates inspired by those challenges.

Professor Andrew Samuels, University of Essex
and Goldsmiths College,
University of London

Contents

Acknowledgements

I would like to thank my colleagues at the University of New England for providing me with an academic haven in which to work. Of these special thanks are due to Dr Robert Haskell, who has provided me with many hours of stimulating conversation about cognitive science, unconscious mental processes and related matters, Dr Samuel McReynolds, former Chair of the Department of Social and Behavioral Sciences, and Dr Jacques Carter, Dean of the School of Arts and Sciences.

During the period of the planning and writing of this book I changed employment twice, moved house five times, and moved from the United Kingdom to the USA. I would like to thank my editor Dr Windy Dryden for his non-interventionist stance as these and other events caused me to be over a year late in producing the final manuscript.

The bulk of this book was written in Grange Hill, Jamaica during the summer of 2001, and thanks are due to all of the people who made my stay such a comfortable and pleasant one. These include my mother-in-law Elaine Stewart, my father-in-law Winston 'Barnsey' Graham and my sister Ann Marie Graham. Thanks also to Marcia, Vinetta, Lorraine, Patrick, Milford, Karlene, Novey J., Deshawn, Tyler, Dwane, LaToya, cane-man Dred and John. Special thanks go to Mrs Ouida Lawrence, who extended her hospitality to my wife and I during the duration of our stay.

I owe a great debt of thanks to Dr Harry Schlepperman, who has generously shared with me his vast knowledge of the history and philosophy of psychoanalysis.

Finally, I thank my wife, Subrena, whose support, encouragement and incisive mind have contributed immensely to this project.

David Livingstone Smith

1
Introduction

Although its fate in the twenty-first century is yet to be determined, even the most vehement opponents of psychoanalysis agree that it has had a uniquely powerful impact on twentieth century thought. For good or for ill, psychoanalysis has fundamentally altered our conception of ourselves and has been rich in ramifications for psychology, the arts, politics, anthropology and virtually every other discipline concerned with human nature.

Psychoanalysis has also given birth to modern forms of psycho-therapy and counselling. Although the psychotherapeutic industry existed prior to Freud, its practices were so crude that it is no exag-geration to say that early psychoanalysts created psychotherapy as we recognize it today. Almost every form of insight-orientated therapy, even those whose advocates most vociferously denigrate the work of Freud and his heirs, has a psychoanalytic skeleton tucked away somewhere in its closet. Fritz Perls, the co-founder of Gestalt Therapy, began his clinical career as a psychoanalyst. Perls under-went analysis with Wilhelm Reich, and later incorporated many of Reich's psychotherapeutic principles into Gestalt Therapy (Smith, 1999b). Eric Berne, the founder of Transactional Analysis, trained as a psychoanalyst under Paul Federn, who had been Freud's right-hand man in Vienna. Berne incorporated Federn's concepts and terminology into his new therapeutic modality. Carl Rogers was influenced by the psychoanalyst Otto Rank. Arthur Janov, the founder of Primal Therapy, began as a psychoanalyst as did Aaron Beck, the renowned father of Cognitive Therapy and Albert Ellis, the creator of Rational-Emotive Behavior Therapy. This list could go on and on.

It is common knowledge that psychoanalysis began with the work of Sigmund Freud in the late nineteenth century. The intellectual ferment out of which psychoanalysis grew is less widely known and understood. Freud was a clinical neurologist who struggled to find ways of treating patients who came to him with functional rather than organic disorders. He wanted to find alternatives to the foun-dationless and sometimes brutal methods of treatment that were standard during the late nineteenth century, treatments such as rest-cures, massage, cold showers, treatment with electrical currents and the surgical mutilation of the genitals. As a neurologist, Freud became an expert on aphasia, a term used for disorders of speech caused by organic damage to the brain. Aphasiology was at the time a dynamic interdisciplinary field, with neuroscientists, psychologists, linguists and philosophers all working shoulder-to-shoulder to understand how language, traditionally regarded as our most distinctively human psychological attribute, was linked to the purely physical matter of the brain. It may well have been his experience as an aphasiologist that incubated Freud's interest in realizing what the philosopher and historian of science Patricia Kitcher (1992) calls his dream of a complete interdisciplinary science of mind.

How does one go about investigating the deep structure of the mind? Throughout most of its history, psychology was a branch of philosophy. When Freud began his clinical work, psychology had only just taken its first halting steps towards becoming established as an autonomous science. Wilhelm Wundt established the first psychological laboratory in Leipzig in 1877, when Freud was still a student at the University of Vienna, and similar laboratories soon sprang up throughout Europe and the United States. Working within the psychological tradition established by Descartes early in the seventeenth century, which held that the mind is wholly conscious and that the most appropriate method of psychological research is therefore introspection, he called his approach to experimental psychology 'introspectionism'. Introspectionism set out to investigate conscious experience by using the methodologies of experimental science, and aspired to bring the scientific rigour of physical science to bear on the study of the human psyche. Despite its fanfare, the introspectionist programme was ultimately disappointing. The psychological laboratories of Wundt and his colleagues never quite managed to deliver the kind of consistent scientific results that were being generated in the laboratories of the physicists, chemists and physiologists.

The failure of introspectionism spawned two important although mutually antagonistic developments. One of these was the behaviourism of John Broadus Watson. Watson responded to the poverty of the psychology of consciousness by sidestepping the mind altogether. In his hands, psychology was no longer to be considered as the scientific investigation of the mind, but was redefined as the science of the prediction and control of *behaviour*. The other was Freud's psychoanalysis, which dealt with the unreliability of conscious introspection by devising methods for investigating *unconscious* mental processes. Psychoanalysis was thus was fashioned to serve three purposes in one integrated package: it was to be a method for relieving psychological problem states, a comprehensive interdisciplinary theory of the deep structure of the human mind, and a method of psychological investigation providing an alternative to the time-honoured method of introspection.

The new discipline proliferated quickly. The International Psychoanalytical Association was established in 1911, and there were soon psychoanalysts practising throughout the world. Psychoanalysis diversified almost as rapidly as it spread. Now, at the dawn of the twenty-first century, there are a number of distinctive schools of thought and practice all rubbing shoulders under the umbrella of psychoanalysis. Lacanians, Jungians (of various persuasions), classical Freudians, British Independents, Kleinians, American Object-Relationists, Attachment Theorists, Psychoanalytic Self Psychologists and Modern Psychoanalysts all adhere to more or less different beliefs and practices, and this list is far from exhaustive.

The lushly variegated character of contemporary psychoanalysis poses real problems for the author wishing to provide a well-rounded introductory survey of the major critical debates. Were I to opt for completeness, I would need to write a very large tome indeed. A complete account of the criticisms that have been levelled at Freud's work alone would exceed the bounds of this volume; all the more so a book detailing the critiques of one another generated by rival psychoanalytic schools of thought. I have therefore had to make hard decisions. My selection of what to include was based on two guiding principles. First, I felt it essential to include the major strands of critical debate directed at psychoanalysis from outside of the world of psychotherapy, for these address the fundamental issues that give the debate its wider cultural and intellectual significance. Criticisms offered from the outside also have an especially incisive character and are, more often than not, applicable with equal force to the non-psychoanalytic therapies. Second, I have attempted to confine myself to what is most fundamental and universal within the broad purview of psychoanalysis.

As a profession, psychotherapy has been extraordinarily bad at self-criticism. The full extent of this was brought home to me some years ago when I was invited to write a chapter on the Freudian approach for a book comparing various forms of psychotherapy, in which each author was required to write, amongst other things, a section on the limitations of their favoured approach (Dryden, 1996). Although some of the contributors did specify pertinent shortcomings, others seemed to regard their approach as essentially flawless. In the section on the limitations of the Adlerian approach, for example, the author humbly informs us that 'Adler's theory of personality provides Adlerian therapists with a complete understanding of all human behaviour' (Clifford, 1996: 166), whereas the limitations of the person-centred approach are merely 'a reflection of the personal limitations of the therapist' (Thorne, 1996: 140) as is also said to be the case with personal construct therapy and transactional analysis. The existentialist approach, on the other hand, is described as being limited largely by patients' inability to make use of it, although the most 'absolute' limitation rests in the fact that few mortals are able to fulfil the extremely high standards required of existential therapists, who must possess the appropriate life experience, exceptional levels of personal maturity and have undergone intensive training, as well as being 'wise and capable of profound and wide-ranging understanding of what it means to be human' (van Deurzen, 1996: 183). Many are called but few are chosen. The pure Light of Truth of psychotherapy is diffracted by the imperfect prism of the merely human minds of its devotees.

There is an almost comical contrast between psychotherapists' idealization of their discipline and the disreputable position that it occupies in the intellectual and scientific world at large. There is clearly something fundamentally wrong with a field whose leading lights cannot locate anything wrong with it. As Karl Popper pointed out long ago, knowledge grows through criticism. If psychotherapy hopes to grow, rather than merely proliferate, its advocates need to abandon their unwarranted conviction that their preferred approach is essentially flawless, and to open their eyes to what turns out to be quite a messy situation.

I am a philosopher and have practised for many years as a psychoanalytic psychotherapist. I have spent the greater part of my working life training clinicians and lecturing on psychoanalysis at a variety of universities in the UK and the US. As a clinician, I have always tried to help students understand psychoanalytic theory and master its technique, while as a philosopher I help them acquire a balanced and critical attitude towards what they are learning. Intellectual responsibility is a burden that not all of us wish to bear. Many, or perhaps most, practitioners are attracted to the field of psychotherapy for quasi-religious reasons. Psychotherapy offers salvation to initiates, who in turn become purveyors of salvation. With these kinds of emotional stakes it can be very difficult to critically analyse the logical and evidential basis of one's beliefs.

It is in this important area that I have encountered a yawning gap both in the literature and in the curricula of training institutions. Criticisms of psychoanalysis are rarely seriously addressed in psychoanalytic education. It is quite possible for students of psychoanalysis to pursue their training whilst remaining blissfully unaware of the serious and substantial critical literature on their beloved subject. This is both poor educational practice and is also morally irresponsible. After all, most graduates of training programmes go on to use their newly acquired methods on real people. It is alarming that students can successfully complete a programme of training in many institutions without even a passing nod at the very real and very serious clinical and theoretical shortcomings of psychoanalysis. Psychoanalysts and psychoanalytic psychotherapists are not usually very well versed in this literature and all too often dismiss it. Ignoring thoughtful criticism is destructive to any discipline. The consequences for psychoanalysis, which has been steadily losing ground in the scientific community, may prove to be disastrous.

The failure of psychoanalysis to engage with its critics goes back at least as far as Freud's injunction that psychoanalysts should not engage in public debate with their critics (Decker, 1977) and his efforts to deflect criticism by attributing it to the emotional resistances of the critic (Freud, 1925). Of course, it is entirely possible for a critic of psychoanalysis to be motivated by resistance and hostility, but the motive of the critic is simply irrelevant to validity of the criticism. We would not dismiss a Jewish historian's account of National Socialism simply on the grounds of his Jewishness, or a Black sociologist's analysis of racism on the grounds of his ethnicity. The validity of a criticism must be considered on its own merits. To fail to do so is to fall foul of what philosophers call the 'genetic fallacy': the origin of an idea has no logical bearing on its truth or falsehood. Ideas should be judged on their own merits.

The issue of emotional resistance is very pertinent to this book and the way that readers may respond to it. My experience in the world of psychotherapy has taught me that, on the whole, practitioners find it extremely difficult to engage rationally with critiques of their discipline. Psychoanalysis is an emotive subject, and discussions of it often generate more heat than light. Advocates of psychoanalysis are likely to find the critical literature rather threatening. To many, psychoanalysis is more than a theory of mind and an associated set of methods: it is a way of life and a road to deliverance. To find psychoanalysis wanting may hold much greater significance for the advocate of the subject than the mere identification of a problem that needs to be addressed: it may be experienced an assault on their identity and the very meaning of their life. With friends like this, psychoanalysis does not need enemies, for in order to grow a discipline needs to actively seek out its own defects. How else it is possible to repair them? Many years spent teaching psychoanalysis, writing on psychoanalysis and presenting papers on psychoanalysis have taught me that it is a rare individual within the field who is able to thoughtfully address such issues. The most common reactions are intemperate rejection and unconsidered denial. As Adolf Grünbaum (1993) has observed:

> Very understandably, those who see their doctrine in jeopardy may find it more difficult to be receptive to my demurrer than it is for me to issue it ... After all, whatever the fortunes of my polemic against Freud's clinical arguments and against post-Freudian variants on them in the marketplace of ideas, my own professional craft as a philosopher is not put at risk by the outcome. (xi)

Grünbaum goes on to make the crucial point that if psychoanalysis is ever to be placed on a sound footing 'it is essential to have a clear appreciation of the range and depth of the difficulties besetting its extant defences' (ibid). This book was written to help students, practitioners and educated lay persons do just this. Much, although by no means all, of the critical literature is intellectually demanding and written in an idiom that may be unfamiliar to non-specialists. This is particularly true of the philosophical literature. *Psychoanalysis in Focus* attempts to smooth the way by providing an accessible and relatively jargon-free exposition of the main issues with, I hope, no loss in intellectual rigour.

There is a different type of reader that may be attracted to this book: the person who is antagonistic to psychoanalysis and is seeking more effective critical weapons to deploy against it, but who is an advocate of some rival psychotherapeutic modality. To this reader *Psychoanalysis in Focus* may be a mixed blessing. It will certainly add hardware to his or her arsenal. On the other hand, many of the critical points - and certainly all of the most profound and far-reaching ones – apply with equal force to other forms of psychotherapy. Let the reader therefore beware of pointing out the mote in his brother's eye without noticing the beam in his own.

From the 1920s onwards, psychoanalysis attracted the attention of philosophers. Philosophers are professional critics, so it is not surprising that some of the most incisive and potentially devastating criticisms of psychoanalysis have emanated from this direction. Chapter 2 of this book scrutinizes some of the major critiques of psychoanalysis framed by philosophers of science from the logical positivists to the contemporary work of Adolf Grünbaum.

Working scientists have also devoted attention to psychoanalysis. Chapter 3 examines the question of whether experimental studies and the results of scientific investigations in adjacent fields have validated aspects of psychoanalytic theory, as well as the question of empirical research into the outcome of psychoanalytic therapy.

In light of the objections raised by scientific investigators, the view has been gaining ground for some time that psychoanalysis should be understood as an interpretative discipline rather than as a scientific project, and that Freud suffered from a dire misconception of the character of his own brainchild. This 'hermeneutic' perspective is the subject of Chapter 4, which will also interrogate its epistemological coherence and ethical implications.

An emphasis on the role of the unconscious has been the trademark of psychoanalysis from 1895 to the present day. Proponents of rival psychological and psychotherapeutic schools have raised a number of objections to the very idea of unconscious mental states. Chapter 5 critically evaluates a some of these objections and then moves on to evaluate critiques of the main psychoanalytic method for accessing unconscious mental contents: the free association method.

Transference and countertransference are at the living heart of contemporary psychoanalytic technique and practice, and as such go virtually unquestioned. Can these concepts withstand close examination? Chapter 6 surveys and evaluates some of the powerful objections that have been raised against them.

Psychoanalysis prides itself on its emphasis on the truth, but how far has this commitment been put into practice? Chapter 7 uses an historical perspective to question the integrity of psychoanalytic practice.

Psychoanalysis in Focus concludes with a chapter that sums up some of the core problems confronting psychoanalysis today, and offers some suggestions about what needs to be done in order for the discipline to resolve them and to progress.

I have tried as far as possible to define psychoanalytic terms and concepts as they arise in the text. However, this is only possible to a limited degree in a work of this kind which must, by its very nature, assume that the reader is in possession of at least a basic knowledge of psychoanalysis. For those who do not possess such a grounding, or who feel the need to augment their understanding of the subject so as to better come to grips with the critical debates presented in the present volume, there are many introductory texts on psychoanalysis available. My own *Approaching Psychoanalysis: An Introductory Course,* which provides a guide both to the work of Freud and selected post-Freudian developments, would be an obvious companion to the present volume.

2
Scientific Validity in Focus

Some of the most powerful critiques of psychoanalytic theory and practice have come from the writings of philosophers, especially philosophers of science and philosophically sophisticated psychoanalysts. Many of these are as applicable to the broad family of insight-orientated therapies as they are to psychoanalysis, and therefore pose significant questions for a large section of the clinical field. Before exploring these critiques, we need to briefly consider the relationship between psychoanalysis and science. After all, if psychoanalysis is not in any sense a science, then the criticisms offered by philosophers of science are actually quite irrelevant and misleading.

Bruno Bettelheim (1983) was one of a number of writers who claimed that Freud never intended psychoanalysis to be a 'hard' science. Bettelheim's argument turns on the distinction made by the nineteenth century theologian Wilhelm Dilthey between the natural sciences *(Naturwissenschaft)* and the human sciences *(Geisteswissenschaft)*, and pivots on the claim that when Freud described psychoanalysis as a 'science', as he often did, he meant that it is a human science rather than a natural science. As a human science, psychoanalysis should have investigative methods, justificatory strategies and canons of evidence that are entirely distinct from those used in natural sciences like biology and physics. It would be simply inappropriate to insist that psychoanalysis conform to the norms of natural science, and it is ludicrous to criticize psychoanalysis for failing to live up to natural science standards.

This 'separate but equal' approach to the standing of psychoanalysis is quite attractive to its defenders because it allows psychoanalysis to retain its dignity as a science without requiring it to conform to the seemingly inappropriate standards of disciplines like physics or biology. Psychoanalysts are therefore free to use research methods that are truly appropriate to their subject matter: the inner life of human beings. Bettelheim's argument has apparent plausibility even without making use of Dilthey's specific distinction, as the German term *Wissenschaft* which Freud used and which is translated as 'science' has a much broader extension than the English 'science'. *Wissenschaft* can refer to *any* systematic body of knowledge, so Freud's claim that psychoanalysis is *Wissenschaft* does not in itself mean that he hitched his wagon to the star of natural science.

However appealing this approach may be, it is exegetically flawed. From a purely historical perspective, it is a mistake to claim that Freud regarded psychoanalysis as a 'human' science. Freud was an advocate of the idea of the unity of the sciences and he rejected the very idea of an essential distinction between human and natural sciences. 'The intellect and mind,' he wrote, 'are objects for scientific research in exactly the same way as any non-human things' (1933: 159).

Granted that the 'human science' view of psychoanalysis cannot reasonably be attributed to Freud, it might still be the case that Freud himself *misconceived* the relationship between his brainchild and the scientific worldview. A number of psychoanalytic apologists have argued for this position, the best known of whom is probably the German philosopher Jurgen Habermas (1971). After all, it is said that natural science strives for reliable, rigorously objective knowledge, whereas psychoanalysis is entirely concerned with the more ambiguous realm of human subjectivity. On the face of it the two are poles apart. Perhaps Habermas was right in describing Freud's stubborn commitment to science as a self-misunderstanding (Habermas, 1971). This argument may seem almost self-evidently true when phrased in this way, but it is flawed by confusion between two distinct meanings of the term 'subjective'. Sometimes we use the term 'subjective' for anything pertaining to a human subject. For instance, when we refer to someone's 'subjective world' we mean everything that is personal to them. Philosophers call this 'ontological' subjectivity (ontology is a term for the philosophical study of existence). Ontological subjectivity is all about being a subject, that is, having a personal or inner life, undergoing experiences and so on, and is one of the factors differentiating human beings (and probably other animals) from, say, horseshoes. Horseshoes do not undergo experiences, they do not have inner lives, and they are not subjects. On other occasions and in other contexts we use the term 'subjective' in quite a different way to pertain to matters of *knowledge*. For instance, we may criticize somebody's stance by saying 'That's just your subjective opinion!', meaning 'That's not how things really are, that's just your belief!'. Philosophers call this 'epistemological' subjectivity (epistemology is a name for the philosophy of knowledge).

Once we are clear about the distinction between these two kinds of subjectivity it becomes clear that although psychoanalysis is concerned with human subjects, this is no real obstacle to its being epistemologically objective. The following example shows why. Think of an occasion when someone hurt your feelings. Having hurt feelings is an ontologically subjective state because it is *you*, a human *subject*, who experienced the hurt. It was also an epistemologically objective *fact* that your feelings were hurt. If feelings, thoughts and other psychological states were not epistemologically objective, there would be no point in trying to understand or resonate emotionally with another person's experience. Empathy would be completely impossible. In order to understand another person's feelings there must be some fact of the matter about what they are feeling.

The logical positivist critique

The objectivity towards which science strives is epistemological, not ontological. In other words, science attempts to distinguish facts from unsupported beliefs. Scientists try to understand the world as it really is, rather than how it is 'subjectively' perceived. The crude dichotomy between 'subjectivity' and 'objectivity' is far too simple-minded to capture these nuances. Freud believed that ontologically subjective states can be investigated in an epistemologically objective way, and that psychoanalysis is an attempt to do just this. Psychoanalysis is not, and cannot claim to be, a 'subjective science' for reasons stated above. It can arguably, but as we shall see not unproblematically, claim to be a 'science of subjectivity'.

The very first philosophers to engage seriously with psychoanalysis were members of the group known as the logical positivists. Logical positivism (or 'logical empiricism' as it was later called) was an immensely influential movement that originated in Vienna in the early part of the twentieth century. The logical positivists believed that a great deal of academic philosophy was, frankly, meaningless drivel, and they were committed to the task of bringing philosophy down to earth by making it more scientific. The positivists believed themselves to be in possession of an acid test to determine whether or not a statement is meaningful. They held that meaningful statements are *verifiable*, that is, there is at least in principle some way to 'check out' whether they are true or false. By the same token, statements that cannot even in principle be verified are utterly meaningless and should be ignored by any rational person. Consider the portentous existentialist claim that 'nothingness lies at the heart of Being'. This statement has an aura of philosophical profundity but, from a logical positivist perspective, it is vacuous. What is Being?

What is nothingness? How do we determine if nothingness lies at the heart of Being? Is there some sort of instrument (an ontoscope?) that could be used for this purpose? Intellectual pretentiousness is dissolved by the corrosive force of a determined insistence on the vital importance of verification.

This approach was based in large measure on the work of the eighteenth century Scottish philosopher David Hume. Hume (1748) wrote in the *Enquiry Concerning Human Understanding* that there are two and only two kinds of truths. Some statements are true by definition. An example is the statement 'all triangles have three sides'. We don't have to actually *observe* any triangles to know this to be true, as is the case with similar statements such as 'all bachelors are unmarried', 'all cats are felines' and so on. Hume pointed out that there are other kinds of statements that cannot reasonably be assessed in this way. In order to assess these, we are required to observe how things really are in the world. If I were to claim that there is a canary sleeping in my jacket pocket, this can only be verified by performing some kind of investigation, for example, looking in my pocket to see whether or not there is a canary inside it. Any statement that requires observation to determine whether it is true or false is called an *empirical* statement.

Scientific theories are empirical statements, but unlike the singular statement about the canary, they are about whole *groups* of things. The statement 'HIV is the cause of AIDS' is a theoretical claim stating that *every* case of AIDS is caused by HIV infection. How can we test whether theoretical claims are true or false? This problem cannot be handled in exactly the same way as the claim that there is a canary in my pocket. In the latter example just looking in my pocket is a decisive test, but it is impossible to examine *every* AIDS victim to determine if HIV causes his or her disease. Even if it were possible to examine every AIDS victim alive at this moment, it would not be possible to examine all of the AIDS victims who have died and all of those who will contract AIDS in the future. This problem highlights the fact that there is an inevitable and unbridgeable gap between a scientific theory and the evidence required to establish that it is true. As a result, scientific knowledge is always somewhat uncertain and open to revision. One way to deal with this problem is to see how often a theory is confirmed in particular cases. If medical scientists examine a large number of AIDS cases and discover that in each case the disease was caused by HIV, it begins to seem likely that HIV is always the cause of AIDS. As more and more confirmations pile up, this conclusion seems more and more likely.

When scientists have accumulated very many confirmations, they may say that a theory has been verified.

Logical positivists approached psychoanalysis with the verification principle in mind and wanted to establish whether Freudian theories are verifiable and therefore meaningful, or whether they are nothing more than meaningless pronouncements dressed up as science. This question was explored by the philosopher Ernest Nagel in a classic paper that he presented at a conference on psychoanalysis and philosophy held in 1958 and sponsored by the New York University Institute of Philosophy. Nagel (1959), addressing an audience of distinguished philosophers and psychoanalysts, argued that to be meaningful a theory has to fulfil three basic requirements: it must be logically consistent, entail definite empirical consequences, and be clearly tied to observation.

Consider a theory that is meaningful by Nagel's lights: Isaac Newton's theory of universal gravitation. A logically consistent theory is coherent: it makes sense and does not contradict itself. Newton's theory provides an elegant and highly consistent account of how physical objects interact. A theory that entails definite empirical consequences is able to make predictions about the world. Newton's theory enabled the astronomer Edmund Halley to predict the time of the arrival of Halley's Comet in the skies over England. Halley used Newton's laws of motion to establish that comets appear periodically, and then used the theory to calculate the elliptical orbit of the comet. In the year 1705 he published the correct prediction that the comet would return in 1758, and the actual return of the comet, as predicted by Halley, was a definite empirical consequence of Newton's theory. Finally, a theory that is tied to observation is linked to the real world. Newton's theory is tied to observation in that it predicts the observable behaviour of objects (for example, Halley's comet). Scientists can observe and measure the behaviour of comets and other objects to determine whether or not they match the claims derived from Newton's theory.

In Nagel's framework, the mere fact that a theory fulfils the three criteria does not mean that the theory is true. All that it means is that it is possible to objectively test the theory in order to find out whether it is true or false. A theory that fails to satisfy the three conditions has an indeterminate status: it cannot be tested, so there is no way to determine whether it is true or false. How, then, does psychoanalysis fare in relation to the three conditions? According to Nagel, it suffers from serious shortcomings. Freudian theoretical terms 'lack ... even moderate precision' (Nagel, 1959: 42), and the relationship between them is 'amazingly loose' (ibid.). Nagel's (1959) concerns about the consistency of psychoanalytic theory have been shared by a number of psychoanalysts. For example, American psychoanalyst Roy Schafer has gone on record that:

> Any student of the psychoanalytic literature will be made aware that there is no far-reaching and exact consensus in any specific area of Freudian psychoanalytic thought – not on instinct theory or ego psychology, not on hysteria or schizophrenia, not on technique or criteria for treatment and termination, and so forth. There is consensus on many important details but not on the broad generalisations and their interrelations. Widely used psychoanalytic terms do not always refer to the same phenomena and do not always have the same relations to other terms. The common language hides the multiplicity of meanings. Too often the fault lies in the fact that psychoanalytic authors have disregarded the scientific necessity of explicitly formulating meanings and connections. (1968: 2)

He goes on to conclude that:

> It all leaves one wondering, what exactly is he … talking about? How does he know? What does this mean? And, at the same time, what exactly am I talking about? How do I know? What *can* I know? (1968: 2)

'Psychoanalysis …', states the psychoanalyst-philosopher Marshall Edelson,

> … has not proceeded very far in systematizing or formalizing its theory … the theory is, I believe, even if one were to take Freud's body of work alone, full of inconsistencies, undeveloped lines of thought, and hypotheses that are contradictory in that at the least they appear to have different empirical consequences. (1988: 269)

The philosopher Frank Cioffi (1974), one of the earliest and most trenchant of the contemporary critics of psychoanalysis, has accumulated many examples purportedly showing gross incoherencies in Freud's reasoning. He informs us, for instance, that Freud claimed that when people spontaneously develop psychological disorders in the absence of external trauma, this is because the amount of libido (sexual energy) in their psyche has increased and has upset the internal balance between drives and defences. But how does he know that libido has increased in these cases? Does he have some way, however crude, of measuring it? Freud himself wrote that 'We cannot measure the amount of libido essential to pathological effects. We can only postulate it after the effects of the illness have manifested themselves'. This begs the question of how he can reasonably claim that an increase in libido causes an outbreak of neurosis, go on to assert that the quantity of libido cannot be measured, and then assert that the quantitative relationship between libido and neurosis is postulated only after the fact? Freud seems to have committed a crude error in scientific reasoning, but in this case the error may be more apparent than real. Libido is an unobservable, a purely theoretical entity postulated by the theory. Nobody has ever seen it, touched it, tasted it or measured it. Many sciences postulate unobservable entities, forces or processes rather like the libido. Physics is full of them. So is psychology. Cognitive psychologists talk about 'cognitive schemas', which are hypothetical mental structures. Nobody has ever seen or measured a cognitive schema and it is unlikely that anyone ever will. Cognitive schemas have a place in psychology because of their theoretical value: they are conceptual tools that help us to understand human behaviour. Furthermore – and this may sound strange to non-scientists – a science is not obliged to regard its own theories as true. There are many physicists who do not believe that the weird accounts of micro-physical reality purveyed by quantum theory are strictly *true*. This does not mean that these scientists are opposed to quantum physics, or believe that it should be discarded. A theory that is not true can nevertheless be *reliable*. This view, which is called 'anti-realism', regards theories as nothing more than effective tools for predicting and controlling phenomena. What matters to an anti-realist is whether or not theories work, not whether or not they are true. Other scientists, who are 'realists' about theories, believe that their theories work because they provide a true picture of the world. According to realism, theoretical entities such as Freud's libido should designate real, although thus far unobserved, entities. A good example is the unit of heredity postulated by Gregor Mendel in the mid-nineteenth century that he called the 'gene'. Mendel could not observe genes, but he needed them to account for his observations of heredity and to predict hereditary effects. Genes were only observed many years later with the development of electron microscopy. Nowadays we know where genes are located and even what they are made out of, and we can use this knowledge to modify and manipulate them.

Freud made his views on the reality of the libido quite clear in a debate with Alfred Adler at the Vienna Psychoanalytic Society. Adler had claimed that there is no such thing as libido, and that the concept ought therefore to be discarded. Freud agreed with Adler that libido is not real, but added that it is 'totally arbitrary and an unscientific conception' to conclude from this that the libido theory is *false* (Nunberg and Federn, 1967: 148–9). Freud was aware that even highly sophisticated scientific theories rely on theoretical fictions, or 'mythology' as he liked to call them (Freud, 1933). As an anti-realist about libido, Freud did not have to square the claim that libido cannot be measured with his use of the concept for explanatory purposes. Although Cioffi's criticism misfires, Freud is not yet in the clear for, despite the fact that there is nothing technically incoherent about Freud's proposals, they can only be only vindicated if they can be scientifically tested. As we will see, psychoanalytic theory does fare very poorly in this respect.

Popper's critique

Karl Popper introduced the next wave of philosophical criticism of psychoanalysis. Popper grew up in Freud's Vienna. He was a childhood friend of Freud's sister Rosa, and as a young man did voluntary work in Alfred Adler's child guidance clinics. Popper called his philosophy 'falsificationism' because it sharply contradicted the 'verificationism' of the positivists. Remember, the logical positivists' touchstone was the principle that only verifiable statements are meaningful. Popper took issue with the principle of verification on the grounds that no matter how many times a proposition has been empirically verified, the very next observation may prove it to be wrong. Consider the classic example of the 'theory' that all swans are white. In order to test this, a verificationist would carefully record observations of white swans, accumulating very impressive statistics on the frequency of white swan sightings. Each sighting of a white swan would be interpreted as support for the theory, making its truth increasingly probable. But does this really make sense? No, says Popper, because the very next observation may be of a black or grey swan. No matter how many white swans one may observe, this cannot possibly demonstrate that all swans are white, but the observation of just one black swan can decisively disprove it. 'It is easy,' he wrote, 'to obtain confirmations, or verifications, for nearly every theory – if we look for confirmations' (Popper, 1963: 36). Popper's point is that attempts to *prove* theories are inevitably misguided. Instead, he counsels, we should try to disprove or *falsify* them. The falsificationist researcher would not shore up sightings of white swans; he or she would seek out non-white swans instead. To put it another way, the falsificationist attempts to prove the inverse of the claim being tested. Rather than trying to prove that all swans are white, he or she tries to prove that at least one swan is not white. There is simply no Holy Grail of positive certainty, no method by means of which scientific theories can be proved to be true. At most, we can legitimately conclude only that despite strenuous efforts a theory has not been proven false. A theory that has not been proven false is said to be 'corroborated' and can be provisionally accepted.

Popper's method of distinguishing science from non-science pivots on the principle of falsification. Scientific statements are statements that are in fact or in principle refutable. As was the case with the logical positivist criterion, Popper allows that a scientific claim may be false. The assertion that the Moon is made out of green cheese is, by Popperian standards, a falsifiable proposition. Astronauts can travel to the Moon and return with samples of lunar material for laboratory testing. A laboratory analysis demonstrating that the samples brought back by the astronauts are lumps of rock and not lumps of cheese proves that the 'green cheese' hypothesis is false. The proposition that the Moon is made of green cheese is scientific not because it is true, but because it can be tested for falsification.

Some systems of thought are woven from theories that seem on the surface to be impressively scientific, but upon closer scrutiny turn out to be unfalsifiable. Popper called these pseudo-sciences 'disciplines that ostentatiously display the appearance of science without its substance'. Consider astrology. Astrology might appear to the layman to be impressively scientific. Astrologers must be competent to draw a map of the sky (a horoscope or 'chart'), which was once done using books of planetary motion ('ephemerides') and logarithmic tables but is nowadays more frequently performed by electronic computers. Making use of a host of techniques, rules and procedures with scientific sounding names – such as primary, secondary and tertiary progressions; solar and lunar returns; transits and midpoints – astrologers make inferences ('predictions' if you will) about the real world. The branch of astrology known as 'natal astrology' attempts to describe the life and personality of a person on the basis of the position of the Sun, Moon and planets relative to the Earth at the moment when the 'native' or subject was born. In order to do this, astrologers attribute certain personality characteristics to those born with the Sun in each of the zodiacal signs. For example, persons born when the Sun is in the sign of Libra are described by astrological theory as being friendly, honest, loyal, original, intellectual, intractable and unemotional. Of course, it is not difficult to find examples of Librans who express the very contrary of these traits. There exist Librans who are unfriendly, disloyal, unoriginal, unintellectual, tractable and emotional. However, astrologers do not regard such examples as falsifying their theory. They continue to assert that

Librans *typically* possess the traits listed above, but add that a horoscope is a complex thing and that there are many other factors to consider, such as the Moon and rising sign, the position of the planets with respect to the signs, the angular relationship of the planets to one another, their relationship to the horizon and the zenith, their placement in the twelve 'houses' and so on. If one were to point to the example of an unintellectual Libran, an astrologer might exclaim, after studying her birth chart, 'Why of course! Saturn is in opposition to the ruler of her ninth house!' In other words, in astrology there is always an escape clause that provides some way of explaining away any evidence that would threaten to refute the theory.

Popper considered psychoanalysis to be rather like astrology, decked out in the trappings of science but utterly unfalsifiable. Instead of transits and progressions, psychoanalysts invoke hypothetical traumas and regressions that are arguably just as scientifically unsubstantial as the concepts of their stargazing cousins. Neither astrologers nor psychoanalysts put their theories on the line by committing themselves to firm predictions and retrodictions *and* admitting that should these fail to 'come off' it means that the theory itself is misconceived. In other words, if one were to ask a psychoanalyst what sort of evidence would prove a psychoanalytic theory to be *wrong*, one would be very unlikely to receive a non-evasive response. In fact, the philosopher Sydney Hook asked this very question. Hook asked a number of distinguished psychoanalysts how one could determine, in any given case, that a child did *not* have an Oedipus complex. Reporting on the results of this informal experiment, Hook described responses ranging from the patently silly (the child would 'act like an idiot') through the personally abusive to genuine perplexity, but nothing remotely adequate was ever provided by his Freudian respondents. Of course, the problem is not just with the Oedipus complex. Hook could just as easily have asked the same question about any number of fundamental psychoanalytical concepts and, I suggest, would have received much the same kind of responses. He might have asked Kleinian analysts how they would know if internal objects did not exist, asked Jungians how they would know if archetypes did not exist or asked followers of Winnicott how they would know if a child's transitional object did not represent the breast. All of these questions interrogate the very core of the psychoanalytic theory under consideration.

Popper has not been without his critics. Although a systematic discussion of these debates would not be germane to the subject of this book, it is worthwhile pausing to briefly consider two such objections.

One criticism of Popper's approach offered by the philosopher and historian of science Imre Lakatos is that however well it delineates an idealized conception of the logic of scientific research, it does not square with how science is *actually* practised in the real world. Lakatos describes scientific research programmes (of which psychoanalysis can be regarded as an example) as possessing a set of core beliefs which are central defining features of the programme and which must not be criticized by persons working within its purview. The inner core of a theory is untouchable. This 'holy of holies' is metaphorically surrounded by a protective 'outer belt' of ideas that can be questioned, altered or discarded as research and evidence dictate (Lakatos, 1976). According to Lakatos there is nothing wrong with this, for the taboo on tampering with the central core fosters and safeguards research. Psychoanalysis, too, has core assumptions that must not be tampered with on pain of expulsion from the movement, and more peripheral elements that can be freely modified by psychoanalytic researchers. When Freud reportedly beseeched Jung on the occasion of their first meeting to make the theory of sexuality 'a dogma' and 'an unshakeable bulwark' (Jung, 1963: 147), he was underscoring that the theory of sexuality is a component of the hard core of the Freudian research programme. The same is true of the theory of repression, which he described as 'the cornerstone on which the whole structure of psycho-analysis rests' (Freud, 1914b: 16). When, on the other hand, he described metapsychology, the abstract physicalistic models of mental functioning, as 'a speculative superstructure' (ibid.), he situated it in the outer protective belt. It might be argued that in asking Freudians his question about the Oedipus complex, Hook was attempting to induce them to question the hard core of the Freudian paradigm, thus placing them in a double bind which *any* scientific thinker would reasonably be inclined to resist. Are psychoanalysts being judged by too harsh a standard and being pilloried for falling short?

The answer to this question may lie in Lakatos's distinction between progressive and degenerating research programmes. A progressive research programme generates novel results: it allows one to understand, predict and control phenomena more effectively than before. A research programme continues to be progressive just as long as such results continue to flow from it. A degenerating research programme, on the other hand, does not produce tangible results. It does not give rise to new and surprising predictions that are experimentally or observationally confirmed, nor does it add significantly to the cumulative growth of knowledge. The strategy of surrounding an untouchable inner theoretical core with a protective belt is justified only in the case of progressive research programmes whose very fruitfulness informs us that there is something sound at their heart. In the case of a degenerating research programme, there is no justification for keeping the inner core sacred and untouchable. There is likely something wrong with the core, which needs to be exposed to scrutiny, modified or possibly discarded entirely (which would, of course, terminate the research programme).

Is psychoanalysis a progressive or a degenerating research programme? Many authors, some of whom will be cited later in the present chapter, have claimed that psychoanalysis has made immense strides since Freud's day. Unfortunately, this sanguine assessment is pure opinion unencumbered by the awkward burden of evidence. As we will see in Chapter 3, there is little or no evidence that psychoanalysis has *any* pronounced therapeutic effects, much less that its therapeutic potency has improved since Freud's day. There is also little or no evidence that psychoanalysis has become progressively better able to predict and/or control the occurrence of psychological phenomena. However one may wish it were otherwise, psychoanalysis has similarly not delivered sufficient goods to merit the status of a progressive research programme. From a Lakatosian perspective it is a degenerating programme and cannot afford to leave its core unscrutinized.

A second powerful objection to Popper comes from the work of the brilliant physicist-philosopher Pierre Duhem. Duhem observed, long before Popper came on the scene, that the failure of a scientific prediction can be due to any number of factors other than the falsity of the theory from which it was deduced (Duhem, 1914). It might be due, for example, to false beliefs about the world that are not part of the theory being tested. It might also be due to faulty experimental procedures or inadequate methods of observation. In short, the failure of a scientific prediction testifies that *something* is wrong, but does not specify precisely what that something is. Does Duhem's thesis rescue psychoanalysis from Popper's objections? No, it does not. The Duhemian critique of Popper is unavailing to defenders of psychoanalysis precisely because the problem with psychoanalysis is not that it makes *false* predictions, but that it is unable to generate predictions at all.

The problem of unfalsifiability rears its ugly head at many points in psychoanalytic practice. Some of the most obvious examples are of the 'heads I win, tails you lose' variety. Freud himself used this epithet in the paper *Constructions in Analysis* (1937). Speaking of 'a certain well-known man of science' who had treated psychoanalysis fairly 'at a time when most other people felt themselves under no such obligation', Freud remarked that:

> On one occasion, nevertheless, he gave expression to an opinion on analytic technique which was at once derogatory and unjust. He said that in giving interpretations to a patient we treat him upon the famous principle of 'heads I win, tails you lose'. That is to say, if the patient agrees with us, then the interpretation is right; but if he contradicts us, that is only a sign of his resistance, which again shows that we are right. In this way we are always in the right against the poor helpless wretch whom we are analysing, no matter how he may respond to what we put forward. (257)

Is this objection actually unjust? No, it is not, unless there is some principled method for evaluating the truth or falsity of psychoanalytic interpretations. This line of enquiry leads us into issues about scientific validation that will be taken up more fully below. For now, suffice it to say that the form of at least some psychoanalytic propositions seems, in spite of Freud's remonstrations, to confirm the objection. An especially rich source of examples is Freud's work on dreams. Freud believed that dreams are ruled by primary process thinking, a kind of irrational cognition which allows that an object, state or situation may be represented by its opposite and that 'in some instances, indeed, it is only possible to arrive at the meaning of a dream after one has carried out quite a number of reversals of its content in various respects' (Freud, 1900: 328). By way of an example, Freud gives the following dream text, brought by a male patient: '*His father was scolding him for coming home so late.*' Freud comments on this dream as follows:

> The context in which the dream occurred in the psycho-analytic treatment and the dreamer's associations showed, however, that the original wording must have been that *he* was angry with his *father*, and that in his view his father always came home too *early*. (ibid.)

One of the most brazen examples of this strategy is Freud's theory of counter-wish dreams. Freud claimed in *The Interpretation of Dreams* (1900) that *all* dreams are driven by wishes, which they strive to fulfil. Some dreams are obviously wishful. 'Dreams of convenience' are prime examples: rather than getting out of bed and getting ready for work, one *dreams* of getting ready for work while remaining snugly under the covers. Some dreams do not seem wishful at all, and may even involve the frustration of wishes. Freud (1900) called these 'counter-wish dreams'. He believed that these dreams *covertly* fulfil wishes on the principle that the non-fulfilment of one wish may entail the fulfilment of another. Freud (1900: 151) records an example brought to him by a female patient whom he describes as 'the cleverest of all my dreamers':

> One day I had been explaining to her that dreams are fulfilment of wishes. Next day she brought me a dream in which she was travelling down with her mother-in-law to the place in the country where they were to spend their holidays together. Now I knew that she had violently rebelled against the idea of spending the summer near her mother-in-law and that a few days earlier she had successfully avoided the propinquity she dreaded by engaging rooms in a far distant resort. And now her dream had undone the solution she had wished for: was not this the sharpest possible contradiction of my theory that in dreams wishes are fulfilled?

Freud's clever dreamer brought him a dream that apparently falsified his theory of the wish-fulfilling character of dreams. Despite appearances, he claimed that this dream too conformed to his theory, writing that 'the dream showed I was wrong. *Thus it was her wish that I might be wrong, and her dream showed that wish fulfilled*' (ibid.). Freud's pattern of explanation here makes it extremely difficult to test the theory of the wish-fulfilling character of dreams. Any dream that seems to contradict the theory can be interpreted as expressing the wish that the theory is wrong. This does not, strictly speaking, make the theory unfalsifiable. Freud's thesis implies that only those people who have been exposed to the wish-fulfilment theory of dreams, and have a motive for refuting it, should produce counter-wish dreams. It would in principle be possible to use Freudian methods to analyse the dreams of individuals who are unaware of the wish-fulfilment theory in order to determine whether or not they too produce counter-wish dreams. But even though the notion of counter-wish dreams is itself falsifiable, there is still no rule for determining if *in any given instance* an apparently non-wish-fulfilling dream is a counter-wish dream or, instead, a falsification of Freud's theory.

The fallacy of arguing from clinical experience

It is very common for analysts to argue that the truth of psychoanalytic theory is amply confirmed by 'clinical experience' and that, given the wealth of clinical confirmations available to any practising analyst or person undergoing psychoanalysis, efforts to scientifically test psychoanalytic theories are at best otiose. This trend can be traced to Freud himself, for when in 1934 the American psychologist

Saul Rosenzweig sent Freud experimental evidence purportedly supporting the psychoanalytic theory of repression, Freud remarked that 'I cannot put much value on these confirmations because the wealth of reliable observations on which these assertions rest make them independent of experimental verification' (MacKinnon and Dukes, 1964: 703). According to this view, then, experimental confirmations of psychoanalytic claims are superfluous or redundant in light of the daily confirmations provided by psychoanalytical practice.

When a critic states that psychoanalytic theory is not supported by scientific evidence, practitioners may retort that it is supported by 'clinical evidence' and that their daily experiences in the consulting room provide the 'wealth of reliable observations' mentioned by Freud. Even a cursory reading of the literature frequently turns up such statements as 'clinical experience confirms ...' when the author wishes to legitimize one theoretical claim or another. Is this tactic defensible? The therapeutic situation can be understood as a sort of laboratory. Perhaps these very special laboratory conditions produce phenomena that cannot be observed in other settings and which dramatically and unambiguously support Freudian theory. This kind of situation is typical of a good deal of scientific research. Scientific theories are often experimentally confirmed in the laboratory under tightly controlled 'artificial' conditions. Someone who does not have access to the laboratory is not in a position to dispute the findings. Freud pressed this point in his 1909 address delivered at Clark University in Worcester, Massachusetts:

> You might be surprised to learn that, in Europe, we have heard a slew of judgments about psychoanalysis given by individuals who know nothing about the technique, who have not applied it, but who disdainfully demand that we should prove to them the accuracy of our results. Of course, among these opponents are those who otherwise are not foreign to the scientific way of thinking, who, for instance, would not reject the results of a microscopic investigation because the anatomical preparation could not be confirmed by the naked eye, but not until they themselves had judged the contents with the aid of a microscope. But in the matter of psychoanalysis, the circumstances are really unfavourable for gaining recognition. (Freud, 1910a: 40)

This intriguing similarity conceals a number of dissimilarities. Scientific experiments are presented with detailed protocols that specify just how the experiment was performed, a practice that enables fellow scientists to critically examine the experiment and to replicate it. Experimental literature also includes detailed accounts of the phenomena produced by the experiment. When psychoanalysts claim that clinical experience strikingly confirms psychoanalytic theory, they do not back this up with meticulously recorded, objective information. The phenomena are at best described in a sketchy, epistemologically subjective and strongly theory-laden manner. Nowhere is this more apparent than in psychoanalytic discussions about so-called 'clinical facts'. In the view of Sandler and Sandler (1994):

> The analytic facts we derive from our clinical work are constructs. As the analysis proceeds we automatically and unconsciously register what we perceive, inevitably in a selective manner. As observers we organize our perceptions, and in this process the unconscious theories and models we have built of the course of years play a central part. Much of this unconscious theory is 'good' theory, that is, it is theory which is effective and geared to reality. (1008)

After quoting this and other similar passages in his book *For and Against Psychoanalysis* (1997), Steven Frosch enquires rhetorically:

> Is this a reasonable account of an exceptional method, built around the detailed exploration of one unconscious by another, and hence exempt from the usual requirements of scientific activity? Is it an approach that might apply to *all* human and social science? Or is it special pleading aimed at covering over scandalous transgressions of acceptable research methodology? (59)

Frosch chooses the second option. My own choice must, regrettably, be the third. Of course, the analyst's personal engagement in the analytic process inevitably introduces or exacerbates cognitive biases. To call these biases a 'theory' and go on to assume, without a shred of evidential backing, that much of this is 'good' theory, does nothing but obscure the problem. Just how much of this work is 'good' theory and how much is 'bad'? What is an acceptable ratio of 'good' to 'bad' theory? More profoundly, given the multiple epistemological handicaps of psychoanalysis described in the present chapter, is it even *possible* for psychoanalysts to make a sound distinction between 'good' and 'bad' theory? If not, what grounds can Frosch or anyone else have for espousing the view that *any* of this is good theory? The remarks by Sandler and Sandler, quoted so approvingly by Frosch, beg the most momentous epistemological question facing psychoanalysis today.

Popper amusingly expressed a second problem with the argument from clinical experience in an anecdote about a supervisory session with Alfred Adler.

> Once, in 1919, I reported to him a case which to me did not seem particularly Adlerian, but which he found no difficulty analysing in

terms of his theory of inferiority feelings, although he had never seen the child. Slightly shocked, I asked him how he could be so sure. 'Because of my thousandfold experience,' he replied; whereupon I could not help saying: 'and with this new case, I suppose, your experience has become thousand-and-one-fold'. (Popper, 1963: 34–5)

Recall that Popper believed that psychoanalysis is a pseudoscience. He held that 'it was practically impossible to describe any human behaviour that might not be claimed to be a verification of these theories' and 'those "clinical observations" which analysts naively believe confirm their theory cannot do this any more than the daily confirmations which astrologers find in their practice' (1963: 37–8). Psychoanalytic theory suffers from excessive versatility: it can all too easily 'explain' any phenomenon that comes its way. Popper went on to remark that clinical observations are nothing more than:

... *interpretations in the light of theories* ... and for this reason alone they are apt to seem to support those theories in the light of which they are interpreted. But real support can be obtained only from observations undertaken as tests ... and for this purpose *criteria of refutation* have to be laid down beforehand: it must be agreed which observable situations, if actually observed, mean that the theory is refuted. (1963: 38, n. 3)

Returning to the anecdote, it seems that Adler simply found some way of interpreting the facts in a way that squared with his theory. Adler, or Freud, or Klein or whomever need only be sufficiently imaginative to fit any clinical observation whatsoever into the framework of their theory. Given the looseness of all of these theoretical frameworks, it is all too easy to explain away virtually any anomaly, just as an investigator trying to prove that all swans are white might deal with a black swan by claiming that the bird in question is not really a swan or that it is not really black (Popper, 1976). David Tuckett (1994), past editor of the *International Journal of Psycho-Analysis*, has noted that 'our standards of observation, of clarifying the distinction between observation and conceptualisation, and our standards of debating and discussing our observations are extraordinarily low' (865).

Cioffi (1974) presents numerous examples of apparent immunization culled from Freud's writings. For example, he points out that Freud claimed that all neuroses are caused by sexual frustration. However, this idea did not seem to be consistent with clinical observations of the so-called 'war neuroses'. Many soldiers returned from the killing fields of World War I with severe symptoms of traumatic stress. These symptoms seemed to have more to do with the soldiers' exposure to the unprecedented horror of the Great War than to sexual tensions. Having considered the matter during the interim, Freud later explained that the war neuroses are only *apparently* non-sexual. How did he justify this theory-saving move? He proposed that the drive for self-preservation, which is threatened by the trauma of war, is ultimately an expression of narcissism, self-love, and as self-love is ultimately a form of sexuality it follows that threats of death and injury are really forms of sexual frustration. This baroque justification of the sexual theory was then supplemented by the extraordinary claim that concussions received on the battlefield are a source of sexual excitement.

Recall that Freud situated his theory of sexuality within the Lakatosian central core of psychoanalysis. One may be forgiven for concluding that he went to extreme lengths to preserve his theory of the sexual origin of the neuroses, and that when the theory was contradicted by an awkward fact he simply expanded the meaning of the term 'sexuality' to cover it. This strategy has a large price tag attached: a wildly over-extended and virtually all-encompassing theory becomes unfalsifiable and scientifically empty.

Grünbaum's critique

Adolf Grünbaum is the most distinguished living philosophical critic of psychoanalysis. A philosopher of science by training, he initially became interested in psychoanalysis because of his disagreement with Popper's falsificationism. He selected psychoanalysis as the arena in which to do gladiatorial battle with Popper. Grünbaum's critique of Popper developed into a much more extensive critique of psychoanalysis itself, which made its debut outside the pages of academic journals in his landmark book *The Foundations of Psychoanalysis: A Philosophical Critique* (Grünbaum, 1984). Grünbaum's writings on psychoanalysis have generated quite a large literature, which gives the reader some measure of their impact and significance. The psychologist/psychoanalyst Paul Meehl has written that Grünbaum has put his finger on 'the biggest single methodological problem that we face' and goes on to specify its grave implications as follows:

> If that problem cannot be solved, we will have another century in which psychoanalysis can be accepted or rejected, mostly as a matter of personal taste. Should that happen, I predict that it will be slowly but surely abandoned, both as a mode of helping and as a theory of the mind. (Meehl, cited in Grünbaum, 1997: 355)

Grünbaum's critique of psychoanalysis is built on two pillars. First, he argues contra Popper that aspects of psychoanalytic theory are falsifiable and that on at least some occasions Freud modified or discarded his theories in response to adverse evidence, and that psychoanalysis is therefore not unscientific by Popperian standards. Second, the clarification of Popper's misdepiction provides cold comfort for psychoanalysis because the scientific credibility of psychoanalysis is undermined by far more profound and devastating difficulties than had been dreamed of in Popper's philosophy.

Like any theoretical innovator, Freud was confronted with the fundamental question of how to determine whether his theories are true or false. He was initially impressed with the way that psycho-analytic theory can bring order out of apparent chaos. A confusing dream, a disjointed string of free-associations, or a bizarre set of symptoms can all be made intelligible through judicious use of the interpretative Rosetta Stone of psychoanalytic theory. The obses-sive-compulsive patient whom Freud referred to as the 'Rat Man', for example, suffered from an intense fear that an urn seething with starving rats would be upturned on his (deceased) father's buttocks, and that the rats would then eat their way into his father's anus. This weird symptom can be given psychological sense when con-sidered in light of the Oedipus complex. Freud (1909b) informs us that it served as a disguised expression of the Rat Man's repressed hostility towards his father. Another example, from the thousands that litter the psychoanalytic clinical literature, is from Freud's account of the treatment of his adolescent patient known as Dora (1905a), who reported a dream in which she visited a railway sta-tion and wandered through some woods. Freud explained that the station and woods represented a vagina and pubic hair, and that the dream was sparked by her sexual attraction to an older female friend. Yet another patient, obsessed with the ticking of a clock, was told that the ticking represented throbbing sexual excitement in her clitoris (1915a). Psychoanalytic theory seemed to almost mirac-ulously generate sense from nonsense. There seems to be no psychological lock, however intricately constructed, that this key can fail to open.

This line of reasoning is technically referred to as the argument from consilience of inductions, a term introduced in 1840 by the British philosopher-scientist William Whewell, but is colloquially called the 'jigsaw puzzle' argument because of Freud's analogy that a good psychoanalytic explanation is like the missing piece of a jigsaw puzzle which fits perfectly with the surrounding pieces.

> If one succeeds in arranging the confused heap of fragments, each of
> which bears upon it an unintelligible piece of drawing, so that the
> picture acquires a meaning, so there is no gap anywhere in the design
> and so that the whole fits into the frame – if all these conditions are
> fulfilled, then one knows that one has solved the puzzle and that there
> is no alternative solution. (Freud, 1923b: 117)

Freud, and others coming after him, proposed that this putative
explanatory power that distils the hidden order in apparent chaos
provides psychoanalytic theory with its solid epistemological founda-
tion. Freud was attuned to the possibility that what he called corroborative dreams, which appear to confirm the analyst's
interpretations, may be 'entirely without evidential value' because
they have been 'imagined in compliance with the physician's words'
(1923b). Freud argues that it is not good enough to try to counter
this objection by appealing to patients' subjective resonance with
their analysts' interpretations, pointing out that their feeling of
'remembering' the events reconstructed by the analyst may simply
be a suggestion-induced false memory. In any case, he notes,
patients only rarely respond to an interpretation with this kind of
personal conviction. Psychoanalysis normally proceeds in a piece-
meal fashion, and it is only cumulative effort that constructs a picture
sufficiently complete to warrant such a response. Furthermore,
psychoanalysts often interpret dreams as expressing ongoing unconscious fantasies rather than repressed infantile memories, in which
case there is nothing to remember. Freud claimed that it is only the
sheer complexity of the jigsaw-puzzle-like 'fit' between the interpretation and the psychological material at hand which gives psychoanalytic
interpretations their credence and demonstrates that corroborative
dreams are not simply expressions of compliance on the part of an
obsequious patient (1923b).

There are two main demurrers to the jigsaw-puzzle argument. The
first was voiced by Paul Meehl (1991a), who as a clinician as well as
a philosopher of science is in an excellent position to point out that
the jigsaw-puzzle analogy is in fact wildly overstated. It is simply not
true, he writes, 'that all the pieces fit together, or that the criteria of
"fitting" are sufficiently tight to make it analogous even to a clear-cut
criminal trial.'

> Two points opposite in emphasis but compatible: Anyone who has
> experienced analysis, practiced it, or listened to taped sessions, if he is
> halfway fair-minded, will agree that (1) there are sessions where
> the material 'fits together' so beautifully that one is sure almost any
> sceptic would be convinced, and (2) there are sessions where the

'fit' is very loose and underdetermined ... this latter kind of session (unfortunately) predominating. (275)

The majority of examples in which the fit is rather loose do not provide support for psychoanalytic theory, but even those cases where the fit is, or at least appears to be, quite tight turn out to be problematic. It is a truism in the philosophy of science that any phenomenon can be explained in an infinite number of ways. I can explain this morning's sunrise as caused by the Earth's diurnal rotation. I can also explain it as due to the Sun's orbit around the Earth (as the ancient astronomer Ptolemy did) or as caused by the boat of the god Ra sailing along the heavenly Nile (as the ancient Egyptians did). I might also generate a more novel explanation: perhaps the brilliant orb of the Sun is caused by light reflecting off of Elvis Presley's sequined suit as he flies heavenward each morning. Such explanations can be generated *ad infinitum*. Although they are all explanations for the sunrise, they are not all good explanations. A good explanation must make sense of a phenomenon, but something more than this is required to conclude that the explanation is likely to be a true one. This is just as applicable in the everyday world of commonsense as it is in the more rarefied domain of scientific investigation.

The same principle holds for psychoanalytic interpretation. The fact that it is possible to interpret any psychological phenomenon in an infinite number of ways does not entail that these are equally sound. In psychoanalysis, this problem bites with a vengeance. The complexity of psychoanalytic data, the ambiguity of psychoanalytic theory and the vast number of interpretative options available make it all too easy for a therapist to construct an interpretation that is highly plausible and yet completely untrue. This issue was raised by Freud's friend and colleague Wilhelm Fliess on the occasion of their final meeting in the year 1900. Fliess suggested that Freud might be projecting his own thoughts into the minds of his patients. As Meehl remarks, Fliess 'went for the jugular' (Meehl, 1991b: 284), and Freud knew it, exclaiming 'But you are undermining the whole value of my work!' (Masson, 1985: 450). In essence, Fliess was objecting that the mere fact that Freud was able to tell compelling stories about the origin and dynamics of his patients' psychological problems was just not good enough to vouchsafe their accuracy. Looking once again at Freud's 'Rat Man' case, we can see this problem in a clinical context, as it does *ad infinitum* in the psychoanalytic literature. Freud explained the Rat Man's 'great obsessional fear' that his dead father would be subjected to the rat torture as a disguised expression of his unconscious destructive rage at his father, but he also mooted an alternative hypothesis that the rat torture represented the Rat Man's repressed desire for anal intercourse with his father. Both of these explanations have a certain plausibility (at least, to psycho-analytic ears), and both make sense of the clinical material. How do we choose between them? One might argue that they are both true, and that the Rat Man's obsessive fear was overdetermined, that is, it was caused by both factors working together and that the obsessive fear was thus a condensation of two distinct unconscious ideas. There is nothing wrong with the concept of overdetermination *per se*. In fact, virtually all scientific explanation treats causation as the outcome of interacting factors. But all of this merely begs the question. After all, it is possible to concoct an infinite number of explanations for the Rat Man's symptoms. For instance, one might claim that the Rat Man's brain had been taken over by evil aliens from the planet Zongo which orbits the star Arcturus many light years from Earth, and who control their human victims by planting fears of rat tortures in their minds. Of course, this explanation is so far out that it lacks any credibility. We reject it not because it fails to make sense of the Rat Man's symptom, but because we have no reason to believe that there is such a place as the planet Zongo, much less that mind-invading aliens from Zongo have succeeded in invading Earth.

Although Freud's jigsaw-puzzle argument failed, he hit upon an alternative strategy that Grünbaum has christened the 'Tally Argument'. Its *locus classicus* is Lecture 28, entitled 'Analytic Therapy', of Freud's *Introductory Lectures on Psycho-analysis* (Freud, 1916–17). Freud begins his discussion with some reflections on the role of suggestion in psychoanalysis. Heightened suggestibil-ity is said to be induced by the psychoanalytic process itself. He states with refreshing openness that psychoanalytic treatment makes liberal use of suggestion in order to accomplish its therapeutic aims. In Freud's view, effective psychoanalytic therapy relies upon the patient forming a positive transference to the analyst. The topic of transference will be discussed more thoroughly in Chapter 6. For now, it can be understood as a reawakened infantile desire for the analyst's love and approval. Freud believed that the presence of positive transference is an indispensable component of effective psychoanalytic therapy. The patient, he felt, would be unwilling to undergo the painful and humiliating process of analysis without being spurred on by intense, irrational wishes. In other words, the positive transference gives the analyst some leverage against the patient's resistances. As Freud succinctly put it in a discussion with his colleagues at the Vienna Psychoanalytic Society, patients relinquish their resistances '*to please us.* Our cures are cures through love.' (Nunberg and Federn, 1962–75, Vol. 1: 98–9). Although transference is described as a universal human disposition, it is said to be enhanced in psychoanalytic treatment.

Now, here is the problem. Freud regarded positive transference as the emotional basis for suggestibility. In other words, suggestibility is rooted in the childlike surrender to an idealized other. In conceding not only that positive transference is essential to psychoanalysis, but also that it is a *sine qua non* for a successful outcome that is actively exploited by the therapist, Freud is left with the problem of how psychoanalysts can ensure that the outcome of treatment is something other than a product of suggestion. Freud was adamant that positive transference is the emotional motor powering *all* effective forms of psychotherapy, including psychoanalysis, and that all persons are disposed to form positive transferences except for psychotics. In the more recent psychoanalytic literature, the empire of positive transference has expanded even further, as most contemporary theorists widely concur that even psychotics are capable of experiencing it, albeit in distinctively psychotic modes. But this very theory places psychoanalysis in a bind, for if heightened positive transference is intrinsic to the psychoanalytic situation, this means that heightened suggestibility is intrinsic to it as well, and if patients inevitably become more suggestible during psychoanalytic treatment, there are legitimate grounds for the charge that psychoanalysis is nothing more than a particularly elaborate and sophisticated form of cure through suggestion. Psychoanalysis is vulnerable to the accusation that interpretations are curative, not because they pinpoint the patient's true unconscious conflicts, but merely because of the immense power conferred upon analysts by the positive transference. Remarks and behaviours coming from compliant, suggestible analysands who regard their analysts' persuasive pseudo-insights as profound psychological truths are obviously unable to provide support for the validity of psychoanalytic theory. The analyst who relies on this method of confirmation, as Freud did, is therefore walking on 'thin ice' because:

Freudian therapy might reasonably be held to function as an emotional corrective *not* because it enables the analysand to acquire bona fide self-knowledge, but instead because he or she succumbs to proselytising *suggestion* which operates the more insidiously under the pretence that analysis is *non*directive. (Grünbaum, 1984: 130)

This idea has considerable up-front plausibility. It may explain why practitioners of different schools of psychoanalysis all manage to get clinical 'confirmations' of their favoured theories. As the psycho-analyst Judd Marmor (1962) has noted:

> Depending on the point of view of the analyst, the patients of each school seem to bring up precisely the kind of phenomenological data which confirms the theories and interpretations of their analysts! Thus each theory tends to be self-validating. Freudians elicit material about the Oedipus Complex and castration anxiety, Jungians about arche-types, Rankians about separation anxiety, Adlerians about masculine strivings, Horneyites about idealized images, Sullivanians about dis-turbed interpersonal relationships, etc. ... What the analyst shows interest in, the kinds of questions he asks, the kind of data he chooses to react to or ignore, and the interpretations he makes, all exert a sub-tle but significant suggestive impact upon the patient to bring forth certain kinds of data in preference to others. (289)

Jungians, Freudians, Kleinians, Winnicottians, Kohutians and so on all adhere to very different and often mutually contradictory theories. As a result, they all make wildly different interpretations, but yet all seem mysteriously to get clinical confirmations. These results cannot arise from their all making true and accurate interpretations, because given their mutually contradictory nature the theories simply cannot *all* be correct, despite the prevalent, politically inspired ecumenicism that is so widespread in the contemporary psychoanalytic scene. Of course, if the interpretations work by virtue of their suggestive power, rather than because of their truth, the mystery is solved. This deflationary thesis is for obvious reasons not very attractive to psychoanalysts. Freud (1916–17) succinctly summed up its implica-tions as follows:

> This is the objection that is most often raised against psycho-analysis, and it must be admitted that, although it is groundless, it cannot be rejected as unreasonable. If it were justified, psycho-analysis would be nothing more than a particularly well-disguised and particularly effec-tive form of suggestive treatment and we should have to attach little weight to all that it tells us about what influences our lives, the dynam-ics of the mind or the unconscious. (452)

In fact, the problem is much worse than Freud envisaged. Psychoanalysis might still be clinically justified as a fine suggestive therapy if it really were 'particularly effective'. Unfortunately, there is no empirical evidence that this is the case. Many analysts *claim* that psychoanalysis is a particularly effective mode of treatment, but so do therapists of all other stripes. Such claims should be given credence only when they are supported by a platform of facts. If psychoanalysis is at best neither more nor less effective than other suggestive therapies, then its expense, arduousness and time-consuming nature would count decisively against it.

Most psychotherapists completely ignore the problem of suggestion. In the *Handbook of Individual Therapy* (Dryden, 1996) mentioned in Chapter 1, the term 'suggestion' is only mentioned once, and that occurs in my own chapter on Freudian psychotherapy (Smith, 1996). This unhappy state of affairs cannot be salved by the claim that the issue is of concern only to psychoanalysis. Although Grünbaum has pinpointed the problem in his discussion of Freud's efforts to validate his theories, the problem itself is pertinent to all of the psychotherapies that claim to be doing something more than suggesting away psychological difficulties.

How did Freud meet the problem? Unlike the vast majority of psychoanalysts and psychotherapists, he did not stick his head in the sand and hope that it would go away. He was alert to its gravity and confronted it directly. Although Freud conceded that suggestion plays a potent role in psychoanalysis, he denied that it is sufficient to dislodge neurotic symptoms, declaring of the patient that it 'only affects his intelligence, not his illness. After all, his conflicts will only be successfully solved and his resistances overcome if the anticipatory ideas [i.e., interpretations] he is given tally with what is real in him'. (Grünbaum describes this as 'epistemologically, perhaps the most pregnant single passage' in Freud's writings (1984: 138) because it is here that Freud describes in a nutshell his major strategy for underwriting the truth-claims of psychoanalytic theory. Furthermore, Freud argues that positive transference is eventually dissolved when its usefulness is exhausted. The analyst interprets the positive transference, helping the patient to understand it as a repetition of infantile fantasies and memories. According to psychoanalytic theory, once the patient achieves a true understanding of the childhood memories and fantasies animating the transference, the transference itself will disappear and he or she will be left with a realistic perception of the analyst, unsullied by the incursion of infantile wishes. Freud states that the analyst must 'constantly tear the patient out of his menacing illusion' by repeatedly showing him that the transference is merely a reflection of the past (Freud, 1940a: 177). So, even if suggestion is able to produce truly psychotherapeutic effects, the eventual dismantling of the positive transference in psychoanalytic therapy provides a safeguard against cure by suggestion, and thus shores up support for the validity of psychoanalytic theory.

This solution fails because of its circularity. Why should we assume that the patient's acquiescence with the analyst's interpretations of his or her positive transference, however heartfelt, is not itself a manifestation of suggestibility? In other words, when a psychoanalytic patient accepts his or her analyst's interpretations of the positive transference and ceases behaving in an overtly transference-like way, how are we to be sure that this is not just another expression of the psychological compliance induced by positive transference? Might it not just be positive transference covering its own traces? As Grünbaum (1984) tersely sums it up, Freud's proposed solution amounts to 'a viciously circular bootstrap operation' (144). It is 'question-begging and self-validating' (ibid). This is not just idle speculation or carping scepticism. Freud's claims about the force and pervasiveness of positive transference, and the more recent literature on the power of placebo effects (for example, Frank, 1973; Grünbaum, 1993) underscore these considerations as pressing and serious.

Let us look more closely at the structure of Freud's argument, as it is spelled out in the 'Introductory lectures on psycho-analysis' (Freud, 1916–17) and in the earlier case study of 'Little Hans' (Freud, 1909a). The first premise is that psychoanalytic insight is *indispensable* for the resolution of those intrapsychic conflicts deemed to be responsible for psychological disorders. The second premise is that *only* psychoanalytic treatment can mediate or deliver such insight. Grünbaum accordingly refers to this two-fold claim as the 'Necessary Condition Thesis' (or NCT for short). The NCT drives what Grünbaum calls Freud's 'Tally Argument' – the argument that because effective interpretations must 'tally' with what is real in the patient, psychoanalytic cure cannot be reasonably attributed to suggestion.

Grünbaum (1984) points out that Freud himself had reason to reject the Tally Argument. Freud was well aware of the phenomenon of spontaneous remission, a term used to describe the disappearance of psychological symptoms without the benefit of treatment (for example, Freud, 1905a; 1926a). The existence of the spontaneous remission of psychological disorders has been amply confirmed by later research. In a famous study, Hans Eysenck (1952) claimed that 72 per cent of neurotics spontaneously recover from their disorder with the benefit of no treatment whatsoever. Later investigations failed to confirm the very high rate of spontaneous remission given by Eysenck, but still gave rates ranging from 25 per cent to 52 per cent. The precise rate of spontaneous remission is immaterial to this discussion. Freud's NCT states that spontaneous remission should never occur, so even a *single* example throws the psychoanalytic argument into disarray and undermines his justification of psychoanalytic theory. If spontaneous remission occurs, at whatever frequency, it is simply not true that it is *only* psychoanalysis that can resolve neurotic problems, and if this is the case it follows that there is no justification for the assertion that psychoanalytic interpretations 'work' because they provide the sufferer with true insight into their unconscious dynamics.

Freud knew that rival therapies produce at least apparently curative effects, as he had practised non-psychoanalytic therapy during the early part of his career and claimed therapeutic successes during that period (Freud, 1892). As late as 1917 he remarked that although hypnotherapeutic cures are unstable, sometimes 'success was complete and permanent' (Freud, 1916–17: 449). A second problem for the NCT is the curative effects of forms of psychotherapy other than psychoanalysis. If it is true that psychoanalytic treatment is indispensable to the resolution of a neurosis, rival psychotherapeutic modalities should not work. On the face of it this is simply untrue. In fact, evidence for the curative value of non-psychoanalytic therapies (for example, cognitive and behavioural therapies) is considerably stronger than evidence for the therapeutic power of psychoanalysis (Rachman and Wilson, 1980).

In light of the evidence documented above, how could Freud sincerely claim that psychoanalytic insight is indispensable to cure? His various pronouncements do not appear to add up. The answer to this question lies in Freud's conception of the nature of neurosis. Freud held that neuroses (a generic term that he used for a large number of psychological disorders) are caused by unconscious conflicts. All of us harbour conflicts in the deeper recesses of our minds, and we are therefore all to some degree neurotic. In some individuals unconscious conflicts become so fierce, or the defences against them so fragile, that the ego can no longer contain them and psychological symptoms result. Imagine the mind as a prison. Repressed ideas are like the prisoners, and the forces of repression are like the prison guards. The prisoners are normally kept under control by the guards. However, when tensions become excessive a prison riot may ensue, in which case the guards are no longer able to control the prisoners. In this metaphor the prison riot is like the outbreak of neurotic symptoms. One way that a riot can be quelled is to call in more troops to suppress it. This strategy simply restores an appearance of order without resolving the underlying tensions. In fact, it may augment them. By the same token, suppressing rebellious unconscious urges may eliminate neurotic symptoms. This does not resolve the problem. It only covers it over. Perhaps spontaneous remission and the therapeutic successes of rival approaches can be understood in this light. Speaking of hypnotic treatment, Freud (1916–17) wrote that:

> Hypnotic treatment seeks to cover up and gloss over something in mental life; analytic treatment seeks to expose and get rid of something. The former acts like a cosmetic, the latter like surgery. The former makes use of suggestion in order to forbid the symptoms; it strengthens the repressions, but, apart from that, leaves all of the processes that have led to the formation of the symptoms unaltered. (450–51)

An immediate problem with this argument is that it seems rather *ad hoc*. How can we know that, unlike psychoanalysis, spontaneous remission and non-analytic 'cures' are merely cosmetic? One response would be to say that this simply *must* be true on the basis of what we know about the human mind. If neurosis is rooted in unconscious conflict, and insight into unconscious conflict is necessary for its resolution, and if psychoanalysis is the only method capable of delivering such insight, it follows that spontaneous remission and non-analytic cure must, in the final analysis, be pseudo-cures which at best merely contain and suppress a problem. This argument is unsatisfactory because it is circular. Remember, Freud invoked NCT in the first instance to provide support for the truth of psychoanalytic theory. Psychoanalysts cannot reasonably go on to justify NCT by invoking the very theory that they are trying to underwrite by means of it! In the absence of real evidence, there is no reason why one should prefer the psychoanalytic explanation of the causal basis of psychological symptoms over and above, say, the cognitive or behavioural explanations of the same phenomena.

If the Freudian critique of non-analytic cures is to be credible, it has to possess some independent empirical support. Freud suggested one such independent criterion when he noted that the removal of a symptom by means of hypnosis often resulted in the emergence of a new, substitute symptom. Grünbaum (1984) defines the hypothesis of symptom substitution as follows:

> If the repression of the unconscious wish is not lifted psychoanalytically, the underlying neurosis will persist, even if behaviour therapy or hypnosis, for example, extinguishes the particular symptom that only *manifests* the neurosis at the time. As long as the neurotic conflict does persist, the patient's psyche will call for the defensive service

previously rendered by the banished symptom. Hence, typically and especially in severe cases, the unresolved conflict ought to engender a *new* symptom. (162)

The evidential fly in this psychoanalytic ointment is that there does not appear to be any empirical evidence that symptom substitution regularly occurs (Fisher and Greenberg, 1996). In defence of the Freudian proposal, it is certainly arguable that the relevant research may not be sufficiently subtle and nuanced. Conventional psychotherapy researchers would probably ignore phenomena that psychoanalysts would count as symptoms, such as an inhibition or a characterological rigidity. It might be, for example, that a person 'cured' of a phobia by a therapist using cognitive-behavioural methods emerges from therapy with a sexual inhibition. Psychoanalysts would regard this as a significant symptom replacing the phobia, whereas the cognitive-behavioural therapist would probably not even notice it. Be that as it may, we are left with the reality that psychoanalytically inspired psychotherapy researchers have not yet demonstrated that subtle symptom substitutions are a regular by-product of successful non-analytic treatment. Furthermore, in order to make their case credible, they would also need to demonstrate that symptom substitution does *not* occur as a consequence of successful psychoanalytic treatment. This is a tall order.

Finally, to make matters worse, during the course of his lengthy career as a clinician, spanning more than 50 years, Freud himself came more and more to doubt that psychoanalysis provides a radical cure for psychoneurosis. Freud's growing scepticism became apparent in his 1926 work *Inhibitions, Symptoms and Anxiety* in which he noted that psychoanalytic treatment can normally do no more than accelerate 'the good result which in favourable circumstances would have occurred of itself' (Freud, 1926a: 154). In 1937, he added to this that psychoanalytic treatment offers neither protection against the recurrence of the disorder, nor the outbreak of another (Freud, 1937). The implications of these brave statements are, as Grünbaum notes, 'shattering' for the Tally Argument (Grünbaum, 1984: 160), for if Freud is right then the whole idea that psychoanalytic treatment pulls a neurosis up by its roots is discredited, and with it collapses his major strategy for underpinning psychoanalytic theory. As it stands, then, we have no assurance that psychoanalytic cures, when they occur, are anything more than placebo effects and it may be that, after all, the mighty edifice of psychoanalytic theory rests on the quicksand of suggestion.

Having demolished Freud's justifications for accepting psychoanalytic theory as true, Grünbaum examines the question of what alternative strategies could be used to underwrite it. The bad news is that psychoanalysis cannot be tested 'on the couch'. Psychoanalytic clinical data is too polluted by the possibility of insidious suggestion to bear the epistemological load of empirical testing. The good news is that there are alternative strategies for scientifically testing psychoanalytic theory.

Why can't psychoanalysis be tested 'on the couch'? It has always been assumed that this is the very best arena for testing psychoanalysis because the clinical situation allegedly provides particularly dramatic and compelling confirmations of psychoanalytic theory. According to Grünbaum, it is the very problem that Freud identified – the omnipresence of suggestibility/positive transference – which renders any such attempt Quixotic. Transference is like an invisible acid that subtly eats away at the scientific value of clinical data: there is always some likelihood that the analyst's theoretical expectations will be communicated to the patient and that the patient will unconsciously shape what he or she says or does to conform to those very expectations. Psychoanalysts' suggestions are sometimes quite overt, but a suggestion does not have to be overt to have an impact and it may well be that the less obvious forms of suggestion have greater impact than the more blatant ones. What appears to both analyst and patient to be a 'good' analysis may actually amount to a *folie à deux*. The analyst's expectations are a covertly contaminating factor that, as Grünbaum notes, calls into question the probity of clinical evidence gleaned in support of psychoanalytic theory.

This does not mean that psychoanalysis is entirely untestable. Grünbaum (1984) notes that there are two alternative strategies that are not vulnerable to the problem of epistemic contamination: experimental and epidemiological research. Experimental research takes the subject off the couch and into the laboratory, where it may be possible to control for confounding variables like positive transference. Historically, the relationship between psychoanalysis and experimental psychology has not been a good one. On the whole, psychoanalysts have kept their distance from experimentalists. With very few exceptions, experimental psychologists have eschewed research into psychoanalytic propositions, perhaps because of the complex and seeming methodological intractability of psychoanalytic theory. Many attempts to experimentally research psychoanalytic ideas have floundered because of poor experimental design. However, the fact that good experimental research into psychoanalysis is difficult does not mean that it is impossible, and a number of researchers have attempted to bridge the divide between the 'two cultures' of psychodynamic thinking and scientific psychology (Erdelyi, 1985; Fisher and Greenberg, 1996; Kline, 1981).

The other avenue open to those who wish to critically evaluate the scientific validity of psychoanalytic research is epidemiological research. Epidemiology is the study of the incidence and distribution of disease, including psychopathology. Psychoanalytic claims about the causes and incidence of psychological disorders are therefore in principle amenable to epidemiological research methods, which also circumvent the problem of suggestion. One example, which Grünbaum used to refute Popper's claim that psychoanalysis is unfalsifiable, is Freud's (1911) theory of the origins of paranoia. Freud claimed that paranoia is caused by repressed homosexuality, arguing that a person who is deeply frightened or ashamed of his or her own homosexual impulses may transform an attraction towards an individual of the same sex into delusions of persecution. Grünbaum points out that if Freud's proposition is true, there should be a decreased incidence of paranoia in communities where homo-sexuality is accepted as compared with communities where it is suppressed. Furthermore, the incidence of paranoia should be especially low amongst manifest homosexuals who are at ease with their own sexuality (for a critique of this proposal, see Edelson, 1986).

In spite of his explicit pronouncements to the contrary, there is widespread misapprehension amongst psychoanalytic writers that Grünbaum has proven, or has attempted to prove, that psycho-analysis is not scientific and cannot be scientifically tested. Steven Frosch (1997), to name but one, mistakenly states that Grünbaum has shown that:

> ... the circularity of psychoanalytic theory is such that it can never be established on a 'scientific' basis, if what is meant by that is a discipline in which immaculate and uncontaminated evidence is available for rational and judicious critical scrutiny. (234)

As we have seen, Grünbaum does not claim that psychoanalysis 'can never be established on a "scientific" basis', but only that this cannot be done using current clinical research strategies. Grünbaum's reser-vations about the scientificity of psychoanalysis stem not from the putative 'circularity' of its theories, but mainly from the difficulty in eliminating placebo effects (suggestion) as a candidate for apparent clinical confirmations. It is not clear what Frosch means by 'immac-ulate' in this context, but of course evidence must be relatively uncontaminated to be scientifically serviceable. Grünbaum argues that epidemiological and experimental research strategies provide sufficient freedom from epistemic contamination to make this a real option. Frosch goes on to add that:

> Psychoanalysis suggests that under the best conditions this would be a pious hope as, given the contradictions and confusions of the human psychological states with which psychoanalysis deals, it is never going to be possible to find an objective place to stand. Reflexivity, reactivity, subjectivity – whichever of these terms is preferred, the 'fact' is that psychoanalysis accentuates rather than obliterates the investment of the researcher or therapist in the material with which he or she deals. (Frosch, 1997: 234)

This passage misses Grünbaum's point almost completely. The problem with psychoanalysis is emphatically *not* due to its researchers being subjectively engaged with it. Many researchers in many disciplines are deeply, even obsessively, engaged with their subjects. Passionate engagement does not preclude methodological rigour and intellectual accountability.

One obvious rejoinder to Grünbaum is to assert that although his criticisms are justified when applied to Freud, they are not applicable to more recent developments within the field. After all, it is alleged, we have come a long way since Freud. There are now numerous schools of psychoanalytic thought and practice – Kleinian, Object-Relational, Lacanian and Kohutian to name just a few – which are seen by their proponents as decisive advances beyond the original Freudian concepts and techniques. Returning once again to Frosch (1997):

> Grünbaum's strategy runs up against the enormous changes which have occurred in psychoanalysis since Freud, in clinical theory and practice as well as in the wider articulations of the theory with social and artistic issues. It also results in a failure to appreciate the increasing sophistication of psychoanalysts' own discussions of clinical evidence, in particular their understanding of its constructed nature. (54)

Schwartz (1996) opines in a similar vein that Grünbaum has 'produced a disputation divorced from … the contemporary clinical and theoretical literature' (505), while for Flax (1981) Grünbaum's verdict makes as much sense as 'throwing out physics because there are unresolved problems in Newton's theory' (564). To press the analogy further, just as the theory of relativity and quantum mechanics have transcended Newton's mechanics, so (the argument goes) newer forms of psychoanalysis have supplanted the out-of-date Freudian version. It is as though Grünbaum is pathetically stuck in a theoretical time warp, tilting at Freudian windmills.

The analogy drawn between Freudian psychoanalysis with Newtonian physics on one hand and post-Freudian psychoanalysis with contemporary physics on the other, is not really availing. Newtonian mechanics has not been discarded. It continues to be used by physicists and engineers to describe the behaviour of what we might call middle-sized objects, the vast expanse of physical reality stretching from the borders of the microscopic to the frontier of the cosmological. Certain of Newton's theories, such as his conception of gravitational force, were replaced by Einstein's theories not because they possessed epistemological deficits, but because of their restricted explanatory scope. The 'we've come a long way since Freud' argument seems to concur with Grünbaum's diagnosis, but goes on to claim that newer versions of psychoanalysis have managed to surmount these early difficulties to such an extent that the criticisms no longer apply. Psychoanalysis has changed, but not in a way that neutralizes Grünbaum's objections.

Grünbaum (cited in Eagle, 1983) has stated that 'the much vaunted post-Freudian versions have not remedied a single one of the methodological defects that I generically charged against the psychoanalytic method of clinical investigation' (32). This issue has been closely scrutinized by Morris Eagle, a psychoanalytically orientated psychologist, who has not discovered any evidence that psychoanalysis has managed to transcend the epistemological problems besetting Freudian theory. Although the content of psychoanalytic theories has changed, the problems remain the same. As far as I am aware, none of Grünbaum's critics have offered anything like a concrete and cogent account of how recent developments in the field have managed to overcome these stumbling blocks, although there is no shortage of hand-waving and vague pronouncements about the purported philosophical sophistication of contemporary psychoanalysis. Until such demonstrations are forthcoming, the 'we've come a long way since Freud' response cannot be taken seriously.

Another response to Grünbaum has involved challenging the very conception of science that he uses to measure the adequacy of psychoanalysis. Critics who embrace this argument typically assert that although psychoanalysis is indeed a science, in the full-blooded sense of the word, Grünbaum employs excessively stringent, ideologically laden 'positivistic' standards when assessing it. Grünbaum's 'reading of the bible of science brings hellfire and brimstone down on our hapless and uninformed psychoanalysts' (Schwartz, 1996: 510). Psychoanalysts are 'cowed' by the physical and biological sciences (512). Grünbaum is depicted as a card-carrying positivist bully bent on intimidating and subjugating weak-minded clinicians. Neglecting the rather lurid, *ad hominem* features of this attack, the main problem is that neither Schwartz nor, as far as I am aware, the other critics who take this tack provide clear methodological principles that are not vulnerable to the weaknesses that Grünbaum has identified. It is not sufficient to take issue with Grünbaum's conception of science. We are owed a logically sound alternative to Grünbaum's approach that is able to cope adequately with the problem of suggestion. So far, no such alternative has been forthcoming.

Not all of the responses to Grünbaum have been attempts to salvage Freud. In fact, both Frank Cioffi (1986, 1988) and Allen Esterson (1996) argue that Grünbaum has been excessively generous towards him. If it is true that for many years Freud used the therapeutic successes of psychoanalysis to underwrite its theory as Grünbaum claims, we should discover that Freud cherished a high opinion of the therapeutic puissance of psychoanalysis, at least during this period. Cioffi and Esterson argue that this is not the case. To give but a few examples, Freud wrote to Wilhelm Fliess in 1900 that 'the apparently endlessness of the treatment is something that occurs regularly' (Masson, 1985: 409). In 1906 he agreed with Jung that one should not place too much emphasis on therapeutic results, and mentioned that he had concealed information about 'the limits of the therapy' from a 'hostile public' (McGuire, 1974: 12), and in 1910 he remarked that only time will tell if psychoanalysis will produce better therapeutic results than the prevailing physical methods (Freud, 1910b). Furthermore, in 1905 Freud published the case of 'Dora' in order to demonstrate the evidential base for his theories, but this case ended in therapeutic *failure* (Freud, 1905a). Even in the *Introductory Lectures on Psycho-Analysis*, where Freud articulates the Tally Argument, he states that 'Even if psychoanalysis showed itself as unsuccessful in every other form of nervous and psychical disease as it does in delusions, *it would still remain completely justified as an irreplaceable instrument of scientific research*' (Freud, 1916–17: 255, italics added). Both Cioffi and Esterson argue that the Tally Argument was less pivotal to Freud's thinking than Grünbaum would have us believe. How, then, did Freud justify his theories? He used nothing more sophisticated than the old, philosophically discredited jigsaw-puzzle argument, coupled with personal conviction.

> What gave him his conviction was the subjective feeling of certainty he experienced when he was deriving his analytic explanations from his

clinical (and non-clinical) inferences. The point is, his methods always *worked*, in the sense that he was always able to come up with comprehensive explications to cover whatever he was dealing with. (Esterson, 1996: 54)

Cioffi and Esterson rescue Freud from Grünbaum only to deliver him back into the talons of Popper. If they are right, psychoanalysis is, after all, unfalsifiable and scientifically hollow.

In fact, there is a clinical research strategy that could, in principle, avoid the problem of epistemic contamination by suggestion. I have argued (for example, Smith, 1999b, 1999c) that a psychoanalytic theory might be tested against clinical data without falling foul of the problem of suggestion if the clinical data is generated by a therapist from a rival therapeutic school. We could, for example, test Freudian theories using data from Jungian sessions. If it turns out that Freudian hypotheses are corroborated, this could not be because of the presence of suggestion because, of course, Jungian suggestions rather than Freudian ones would, if anything, taint the therapy. The practical problem with this strategy is that most psychoanalytic theories are not sufficiently robust to be tested in this manner. It is difficult to envisage just how, say, a Kleinian could use her theory to make predictions about phenomena occurring in, say, Gestalt Therapy in a sufficiently disciplined manner for this to serve as a genuine scientific test. To my knowledge, only the communicative approach to psychoanalytic psychotherapy is testable in this fashion.

As we have seen, philosophical critics of psychoanalysis have raised extremely serious charges about the methodological integrity of psychoanalysis. If psychoanalysis is to retain any intellectual credibility, these charges must be faced squarely. Unfortunately, most advocates of psychoanalysis have chosen either to entirely ignore these issues or to content themselves with patently inadequate responses. Marshall Edelson is one of the rare psychoanalytic writers who has honestly grappled with the problems raised by Nagel, Popper, Grünbaum and other philosophers. Edelson (1986) counsels analysts to take a positive, constructive stance and to use the philosophical critiques to help psychoanalysis to get its act together. He makes eight eminently sensible recommendations to psychoanalytic writers which, if implemented, would provide a 'hopeful beginning' (233) to the project of reforming the discipline. Edelson's recommendations provide a 'minimal set of standards' for the presentation of clinical case studies.

- *The author should clearly and prominently state his or her hypothesis, generalization or conclusion about the case. The* reader is in no position to evaluate a claim unless he or she has a clear conception of just what the author is proposing. This problem is particularly acute when considering psychoanalytic case studies which, because of their necessarily labyrinthine structure, may distract the reader's attention from the author's major empirical hypotheses.

- *The author should demonstrate that his or her hypothesis may account for the specific phenomenon under consideration.* Once the reader understands the author's hypothesis, he or she is in a position to consider its explanatory adequacy. Does the proposed explanation actually engage with the phenomenon under consideration? Does it sufficiently address all of its relevant features? Has the author made it clear just *how* the hypothesis accounts for the phenomenon?

- *The author should carefully distinguish facts and observations from conjectures and interpretations.* A clear distinction between *explanandum* and *explanans*, the phenomenon to be explained and the explanation for it, is vital to any scientific endeavour. The failure to consistently make this distinction is one of the most pervasive and insidious problems in the psychoanalytic literature. Terms like repression, fragmentation, reaction formation, unconscious conflict and even (as we shall see in Chapter 6) transference are theoretical terms. They are explanatory rather than descriptive. Consider a situation in which a person forgets a name. Strictly speaking, it is incorrect to describe this as an episode of repression. 'Repression' is an hypothesis about the cause of the forgetting, namely that this instance of forgetting was motivated by the unconscious desire to avoid an experience of unpleasure. To treat repression as a phenomenon is to put the explanatory cart before the phenomenological horse. Nevertheless, psychoanalytic case studies, from Freud onward, routinely fudge the distinction.

- *The author should specify the kind of observations that would falsify his or her hypothesis.* Is the hypothesis falsifiable? If not, then it is not worthy of consideration, but if it is falsifiable the reader is owed an explicit statement specifying just what observations would prove the hypothesis wrong. This requirement is virtually never met in psychoanalytic writings.

- *The author should report at least some observations that seem to contradict his or her hypothesis, and suggest how the anomalies are to be dealt with.* Almost all scientific theories encounter anomalies, phenomena that simply do not behave the way that the theory says they should. It is tempting, although irrational, to pretend that anomalies do not exist, and that the universe conforms perfectly to one's theory. There are several ways that anomalies can reasonably be dealt with. One approach is to argue that the phenomenon in question is only apparently anomalous, and that when understood more deeply it conforms to the theory rather than contradicting it. As we have seen, this is the way that Freud handled the problem of counter-wish dreams.

- *The author should address rival explanations for the phenomenon under consideration, and explain why his or her preferred hypothesis is preferable to competing ones.* As we have seen, there are many possible ways of attempting to explain any psychological phenomenon. According to Edelson, psychoanalytic writing should address plausible competing hypotheses and demonstrate why the author's hypothesis is superior to them.

- *The author should consider whether there are factors at work that may be responsible for a pseudo-corroboration of his or her hypothesis.* Even though the author's hypothesis appears to be corroborated, this may be for reasons that are quite extraneous to the hypothesis itself. Consider the case of a folk-pharmacologist who believes that headaches are caused by a 'darkness of spirit' and that ingesting white substances will therefore ameliorate headaches. This hypothesis entails the prediction that white pills, such as aspirin, will relieve headaches. The folk-pharmacologist decides to test his hypothesis by giving aspirin to a group of headache sufferers and a black placebo to a control group. When the results are analysed, it is clear that the subjects who took aspirin experienced far greater relief than those who ingested the placebo. Does this mean that the original hypothesis about the cause and cure for headaches has been confirmed? Of course not!

- *Finally, the author should make clear the extent to which he or she regards their result as generalizable to other cases, and the grounds for making any such generalization.* Induction, the process of drawing general conclusions from particular instances, is always tricky. Today (Friday) a book fell off my desk. Last Friday exactly the same thing happened, but this does not give me licence to claim that it is a law of nature that books fall off my desk on Fridays. Psychoanalysts attempting to draw general conclusions from particular clinical experiences need to be appropriately cautious in doing so. This has certainly not been the case in the history of the discipline, where sweeping generalizations are often made on the basis of remarkably few observations.

Philosophers of science do a good deal of thinking about science, but the vast majority of them do not actually *do* scientific research.

Perhaps support for psychoanalysis can be found in contemporary scientific practice. What about the efforts to experimentally test psychoanalytic ideas mentioned above? Might not recent developments in psychology and neuroscience corroborate at least some psychoanalytic claims? What of scientific investigations into therapeutic outcome? It is to these issues that we will now turn.

3
Scientific Support and Therapeutic Outcome in Focus

Psychoanalysis does not have a good reputation within the scientific community. In fact, it is probably true that the majority of professional scientists who have an opinion on the matter hold that psychoanalytic theory and its associated methodologies have lost all credibility. The psychoanalysts themselves have, to a great extent, eschewed scientific methodology as is exemplified by Freud's lukewarm reception of Saul Rosenzweig's experimental research mentioned in Chapter 2. For this reason, psychoanalysis is sometimes diagnosed as *anti*-scientific rather than merely *non*-scientific. According to neuroscientist J. Allan Hobson, whose work centres on the neuropsychology of dreaming, the popularity of Freudian theory has actually 'aborted an emerging experimental tradition' of research into dreaming and has been 'impressively obstructive to integrative theorising' (Hobson, 1988: 50–51). The sentiments of many scientific commentators were succinctly summed up by Nobel laureate Sir Peter Medawar, who wrote in a passage that has been cited countless times by critics of psychoanalysis that 'The opinion is gaining ground that doctrinaire psychoanalytic theory is the most stupendous intellectual confidence trick of the twentieth century' (Medawar, 1982: 140). Another Nobel laureate, F.A. Hayek (1978), has suggested that the twentieth century will be seen, in retrospect, as an age of superstition, mainly connected with the names of Karl Marx and Sigmund Freud.

Oddly, it is the discipline of psychology that seems to have the lowest regard for psychoanalysis. Psychoanalysis is something of an embarrassment for psychology because although Freud was not a professional psychologist, and is seen by the profession as a particularly benighted specimen of anti-empiricism, in the eyes of the general public he is perceived as a great (if not the greatest) psychologist. Freud's theories are reluctantly mentioned in introductory textbooks on psychology, although they are often presented inaccurately. Freud's towering intellectual stature makes it impossible for these authors to ignore him entirely, but the references are amply hedged about by cautionary remarks to the effect that this rubbish is no longer taken seriously. 'Freud,' writes Barry Richards (1989: 76), 'is not the only psychologist who is dead. Yet somehow, as one scans introductory psychology texts, he seems to be more dead than others.'

And yet, not all scientists are negatively disposed towards psychoanalysis. In particular, there has been a resurgence of interest in psychoanalysis by neuroscientists. Susan Greenfield, a distinguished British neuropharmacologist, has expressed admiration for Freud as a scientific pioneer, as have her colleagues Floyd Bloom, the editor in chief of *Science*, the veteran neurobiologist Eric Kandel, Nobel laureate Gerald Edelman (Horgan, 1999) and the well-known neuroscientist Oliver Sacks (1988). The distinguished neuroscientist Jaak Panksepp (2000) forecasts the convergence of psychoanalysis with a neuro-evolutionary understanding of cognitive and affective processes, while Nobel laureate Eric Kandel (1998) forecasts that 'the future of psychoanalysis, if it is to have a future, is in the context of an empirical psychology, abetted by imaging techniques, neuro-anatomical methods, and human genetics. Embedded in the sciences of human cognition, the ideas of psychoanalysis can be tested, and it is here that these ideas can have their greatest impact' (468).

The rising tide of interest in the interface between psychoanalysis and neurology was spearheaded by the psychoanalyst/neuroscientist Mark Solms, whose journal *Neuro-psychoanalysis* provides a forum for interdisciplinary discussion and includes a number of eminent neuroscientists on its editorial board. This association should not be surprising. Freud began his professional life as a neurologist and always hoped that psychoanalytic theory would one day prove to be reducible to neurophysiology. Freud incorporated the neuroscientific knowledge of his day into the deep structure of psychoanalytic theory. Furthermore, it is becoming increasingly clear that Freud's work prefigured, and sometimes anticipated, later ideas in neurology and cognitive science, for which he has not been given adequate credit (Smith, 2000).

What kind of endorsement do the scientific friends of psychoanalysis provide? They certainly do not proclaim the truth of psychoanalytic theories. This would be intellectually irresponsible for reasons made clear in the preceding chapter. The scientific friends of psychoanalysis tend to admire Freud for his brilliant theoretical imagination, while his enemies fault him for his lack of methodological rigour. In fact, as the philosopher of science Hans Reichenbach underscored over half a century ago, both creativity (which he called the 'context of discovery') and methodological discipline (which he called the 'context of justification') are vital to the scientific enterprise. Psychoanalytic theorists have been very strong on creativity, but extremely weak on devising strategies for testing these bursts of imagination against data and discarding those which do not meet the test.

The scientific friends of psychoanalysis tend to regard it as *heuristically* valuable. A heuristically valuable theory is a theory whose value lies in its capacity to guide and inspire research. Heuristically valuable theories do not have to be correct. In fact, they can be wildly wrong. For example, Franz Gall's theory of phrenology, the idea that a specific set of psychological 'faculties' are seated in a specific set of neuroanatomical loci, was wildly and ludicrously wrong but was nonetheless valuable because it inspired serious research into the localization of mental functions in the brain.

The scientific investigation of psychoanalytic claims

There are two general ways that scientists have gone about investigating psychoanalysis. One is the investigation of psychotherapeutic outcomes. The other is to design experiments that test specific psychoanalytic claims. These two approaches are to a great extent logically independent of one another. It might turn out that experimentation generously confirms psychoanalytic propositions about how the mind works but outcome research reveals that the therapy is quite useless. Alternatively, outcome research might reveal an enviable therapeutic track record but experimental evidence might show that psychoanalytic propositions about the mind and its depths are deeply misguided. In both cases the *pragmatic* question of whether or not the therapy works needs to be differentiated from the *epistemological* question of whether or not the theory is true or, more modestly, whether or not it reliably predicts psychological phenomena. As we have seen, the good news is that there is now a substantial scientific and experimental literature with a bearing on psychoanalysis, including direct attempts to experimentally evaluate psychoanalytic theories, and that the results of at least some of these studies are strongly suggestive. The bad news is that not one of these studies provides straightforward, unproblematic corroboration for specific psychoanalytic hypotheses and that many of them are handicapped by severe methodological shortcomings. The fact is that psychoanalytic theory is very difficult to test, partly because of its fundamental vagueness (as we have seen, psychoanalytic propositions often do not have clear empirical consequences deducible from them) and partly because of the complexity of the psychoanalytic perspective. Research has neither proven psychoanalytic theory false, nor has it provided dramatic confirmation. Although there has been a measure of debate about where the weight of this evidence lies, even those scientists favourably disposed towards psychoanalysis regard it as inconclusive.

The relevant research literature is both extensive and rather technical, and little purpose would be served by attempting to review it systematically in the present text. The reader wishing to pursue the matter further can consult any of several reviews in the literature, of which Edward Erwin's *A Final Accounting: Philosophical and Empirical Issues in Freudian Psychology* (1996) is perhaps the most sophisticated. Of course, direct testing is not the only way to evaluate the scientific status of psychoanalytic ideas. An alternative and potentially more fruitful approach is to enquire into whether or not psychoanalytic ideas have been independently validated, or at least supported, by recent research in other scientific disciplines. It is to this question that we will now turn.

Cognitive science

As we have seen in Chapter 1, the science of psychology differentiated itself from philosophy and became a discipline in its own right in the closing decades of the nineteenth century. Many of the early psychologists believed that mental life consisted entirely of conscious states, and that the very idea of an unconscious mental state is a contradiction in terms. The failure of this introspectionistic version of psychology to produce significant scientific results provided the intellectual soil in which behaviourism germinated, grew and eventually blossomed. The behaviourists asserted that psychology must be based on the study of publicly observable behaviours rather than private mental states, and therefore rejected the unconscious as being every bit as 'mentalistic', and therefore scientifically unacceptable, as the psychology of consciousness. Behaviourism remained an unshakable dogma amongst the great bulk of Anglophone psychologists until the 1970s, when the new movement of cognitive psychology came into its own. Cognitive psychology made mental processes once again the legitimate subject matter for psychology by stressing the centrality of purely internal, unobservable cognitive states for any comprehensive theory of human psychology. Proponents of the new psychology joined forces with linguists, philosophers, computer scientists and neuroscientists to create the interdisciplinary field of cognitive science: a heady mix that strove to understand the human mind simultaneously from a whole range of scientific perspectives. Psychologists studied the mental processes themselves, while neuroscientists were concerned with their physiological underpinnings; philosophers were concerned both with methodological issues and with the best ways to conceive of mental processes and computer scientists studied how mental processes can be simulated, or even re-created, in silicon brains.

Karl Lashley, a brilliant physiological psychologist to whom many present-day cognitivists trace their scientific lineage, noted that the machinery of mind operates for the most part outside of consciousness (Lashley, 1950). If the mind is compared to a computer, consciousness resembles the screen upon which information is displayed. The monitor screen does not do any work: it only makes information available to the user. The real work goes on out of sight, deep inside the processing unit. Although many cognitivists hesitated to go as far as Lashley, the idea of unconscious mental processes is generally accepted in this field.

Because of the strong emphasis placed by many cognitive scientists on the fundamental role played by unconscious processes in human cognition, some commentators have suggested that this research validates at least some elements of psychoanalytic theory. After all, psychoanalysis has always claimed that the influence of the unconscious is both all-powerful and all-pervasive, and now cognitive science finds that the deep structure of the mind is radically unconscious. The two disciplines seem to be if not identical, then at least fraternal twins (Shevrin, 1992). It is tempting for proponents of psychoanalysis to argue that cognitive scientists have scientifically validated a fundamental psychoanalytic proposition. But this conclusion is unwarranted because the conception of the unconscious held by cognitive science is, to say the least, rather different than that of the psychoanalysts, a situation that led John Kihlstrom to introduce the term 'cognitive unconscious' to differentiate it from the 'dynamic' unconscious of the Freudians and post-Freudians (Kihlstrom, 1987). Although Freud's unconscious is cognitive in nature (Freud explicitly *rejected* the idea that there could be any such thing as unconscious emotions or unconscious drives), a substantial number of psychoanalysts do not conceive of the unconscious in cognitive terms, and even when talking about unconscious cognition, psychoanalysts refer to mental phenomena of a very different order from those studied by cognitive scientists (Eagle, 1987). Cognitive scientists almost always study mental states that are unrelated to emotion and conflict, and which are incapable of becoming conscious because of their very nature, whereas psychoanalysts are usually concerned with conflict-laden, emotionally charged unconscious fantasies and memories that are actively excluded from consciousness by the force of repression.

Consider, by way of an illustration of the cognitivist conception of the unconscious, David Marr's account of how the brain unconsciously processes visual information as presented in his landmark book *Vision* (1982). First, the light striking the photosensitive cells of the retina is converted into an information-structure that Marr represents as a two-dimensional array of intensities, which can be modelled by a numerical matrix. The matrix is composed of units called 'pixels', and the entire array is composed of 1000×1000 pixels. This process generates a 'grey-level image'. The next task is identifying the location of the regions of intensity changes, which involves eliminating extraneous factors or 'noise'. This is modelled by replacing the values of the individual pixels by local averages, using a mathematical operation called 'convolution'. The juxtaposition of these local averages mathematically represents the different regions of light intensity projected onto the retina. The steepness of the gradient between adjacent areas of the array is represented by the use of a simple mathematical formula, which reveals the boundaries between these areas: the local high-points in the values of gradient intensity called 'zero-crossings'. In order to do this, it is necessary to make use of intensity filters of various sizes. Next, the brain compares filtered images with one another, generating three types of shape: 'bars', 'edges' and 'blobs'. The properties of these shapes such as position, orientation, contrast, length and width are all numerically represented in the model. Marr calls this level of visual processing the 'primal sketch'. Next, the images generated in each eye are fused together into a single, three-dimensional image. According to Marr, this is accomplished by the use of innate, unconscious information-processing rules that constrain how the two images are mapped onto one another. One such rule, the 'uniqueness constraint', dictates that each point on one image is to be mapped onto one, and only one, point on the other image, while the continuity constraint states that adjacent points on an image represent surfaces of roughly equal depth. Possible points of fusion between the two images are represented by an array of processors, which are mutually activating and inhibiting. This step culminates in what Marr calls the 'two-and-a-half dimensional sketch', which is based on stereopsis, contour, motion and other cues. The entire process described above occurs in less than a second. We are not aware of performing these complex mental operations, and no matter how strenuously we introspect we cannot observe them taking place. They happen entirely unconsciously. All that we are conscious of is the end result: the experience of seeing something. Marr's story of unconscious processes contrasts sharply with the psychoanalytic version, which is, in the words of cognitive neuroscientist Joseph LeDoux, a 'darker, more malevolent place where emotionally charged memories are shipped to do mental dirty work' (LeDoux, 1996: 29–30). Perverse infantile sexual urges, the horrors of the Kleinian paranoid-schizoid position and other psychoanalytic fare are kept out of consciousness because of the anguish that they would bring in their wake. Marr's visual computations are not unconscious because of any *motive*: they are unconscious because that's the way they are. The cognitive unconscious is analogous to the functioning of a liver. We are not aware of the working of our livers, not because these are repressed or otherwise censored from the slate of consciousness; our unconsciousness of our livers is just an aspect of our design.

Not all cognitive research is so far removed from the concerns of psychoanalysts, and some of it bears directly upon them. There have been a relatively small number of highly suggestive experiments that at least apparently address the interface between psychoanalysis and cognitive science. Consider the experimental study of perceptual defence. A printed word is presented to the experimental subject very briefly using a device called a tachiscope. Words must be presented for a certain length of time before a subject is able to consciously recognize them. However, there are interesting differences in the length of exposure time required before individual words are consciously recognized. Experiments have shown that in many cases words with a negative emotional charge take longer to recognize than neutral or positive words. Although there has been considerable debate in the psychological literature (Brown, 1961; Dixon, 1971; Holender, 1986), the outcomes of these experiments have been widely interpreted to imply that unconscious defences are responsible for the longer exposure time required for the conscious recognition of negatively-toned words. The words are apparently unconsciously recognized, and 'blocks' are then set up against the disturbing stimulus emerging into consciousness.

Even more suggestive is the experimental evidence garnered by the American neuroscientist Benjamin Libet (Libet et al., 1979; Libet, 1985). In one experiment, Libet attached electrodes to his subject to measure the electrical tension that accumulates in the brain when one prepares to perform an action ('readiness potentials'). Next, he asked them to press a button whenever they felt like doing so, and to mentally note the precise time when they formed the intention to press the button (a rapidly-moving clock was provided for this purpose). Libet's results were startling. He found that the brain begins to prepare for the action *unconsciously* more than a third of a second *before* the subject consciously decides to push the button! The experiment clearly suggests that the decision to press the button, an apparent act of conscious free will, was actually made unconsciously.

Do these results, and others like them, provide support for the psychoanalytic concept of the unconscious? They are certainly compatible with psychoanalytic ideas. If nothing more, they show that psychoanalysts are right to assert that mental processes occur outside of consciousness. But this in itself is very weak support, if indeed it can reasonably be regarded as support at all. To understand why, consider the following analogy. The Biblical *Book of Genesis* states that God created human beings after the birds of the air, the beasts of the field and the fish of the sea. Modern biology also claims that human beings came into existence more recently than fish, birds and other mammals. These facts do not provide scientific validation for the Biblical account of creation because although there is a loose similarity between the two, there is also a high level of incompatibility. If scientists discovered that the Earth was created in precisely seven days, that the Earth was created before the Sun, that the first woman was made out of the first man's rib, and so on, this would provide significantly stronger support for the Biblical account, although it would still fall short of fully validating it. The question then arises as to just how close the cognitive scientific account of the unconscious comes to the psychoanalytic version. Does cognitive science offer real evidential support, or is it more like the relationship between biology and *Genesis*?

As Erwin (1996) points out, experiments like the ones mentioned above may reasonably be interpreted to show that (a) there exist unconscious mental processes, and that (b) these unconscious processes influence behaviour. However, this broad statement does not *differentially* support any *specifically* psychoanalytic hypotheses about the nature of these processes and their relationship to human behaviour. To put it another way, there is experimental evidence that is compatible with psychoanalytic theory but which is also compatible with plausible non-psychoanalytic alternative theories, and so long as the weight of empirical evidence fails to support some particular theory in favour of its genuine rivals, it does not make sense to claim that the evidence supports the theory in question (Erwin, 1996). It should also be borne in mind that the vast bulk of psychoanalytic theory remains either unsupported or actually contradicted by the available experimental evidence: this includes the theory of slips, dreams, infantile development, neurotic symptoms, character formation and all of the other domains about which psychoanalytic theory makes particular and detailed claims, including the crucial hypothesis of repression which Freud (1914b) described as the very 'cornerstone' upon which the entire structure of the psychoanalytic edifice rests. Although decisive experimental support for the repression hypothesis would fall far short of validating psychoanalytic theory as a whole, if his estimate of the centrality of repression is correct it would at the very least establish some *prima facie* plausibility for those aspects of psychoanalytic theory that are logically dependent upon it. On the other hand, if the idea of repression were to be experimentally refuted, this would, or at least should, have a devastating impact on most versions of psychoanalytic theory.

Although these investigations provide a useful beginning, psychoanalysis requires a different kind of evidence if it wishes to lean on cognitive science for support. One of the obstacles to realistically assessing the significance of experimental investigations of the dynamic unconscious are the contrived and counterproductive features of the experimental designs themselves. Psychoanalytic theory is concerned with emotionally significant or 'hot' cognition (Abelson, 1963), but as Haskell (1999) remarks, with regard to the experimental study of parapraxes ('Freudian slips'), such experiments suffer from (a) a failure to use emotionally charged material, (b) the failure to situate the experiment itself in an emotionally significant social context, and (c) the failure to make use of material that is of ongoing emotional concern to the subjects. Predictably negative results solicited under such circumstances must be treated with considerable caution but, as Haskell forlornly notes, 'for many cognitive scientists, if an effect can't be reproduced in a laboratory setting, then it does not exist' (Haskell, 1999: 318).

One of the most fascinating of those rare studies that do not fall foul of Haskell's objections was an experimental investigation of homophobia conducted by Adams et al. (1996), which explored the relationship between men's professed sexual preferences and physiological measures of their level of sexual arousal. In this experiment, two groups of heterosexual men were shown a variety of erotic videos. One of the groups consisted of homophobic men; that is, men who reported feeling discomfort, disgust or anger when in the presence of overtly homosexual men. The second group was composed entirely of non-homophobes. Each group was shown a variety of erotic videos, some of which depicted heterosexual sex, others lesbian sex and yet others gay sex. Each man was also attached to an instrument called a plethysmograph, which is a device that monitors sexual arousal by measuring changes in the circumference of the penis. It is unsurprising to know that the plethysmographic readings demonstrated that both groups of men were sexually aroused by the lesbian and heterosexual videos, but the more interesting finding was that it was only the homophobic men who responded sexually to the homosexual videos. Yet, in spite of an unambiguous increase in the size of their penises while watching films of sexual encounters between men, all of the homophobic men subsequently claimed that the homosexual videos did not arouse them. Although from a commonsense perspective these results are starkly counterintuitive, they are actually predicted by psychoanalytic theory, which claims that the homophobe is a person who is so ashamed of his homosexual inclinations, that he sets up a 'reaction formation' against them; that is, he unconsciously represents his interest in participating in gay sex into its polar opposite, an attitude of repugnance toward homosexuality. According to Freudian theory, this conscious repugnance coexists with unconscious homosexual desires, which in this experiment were cleverly accessed by means of the plethysmograph.

Evolutionary psychology

There is no doubt that Freud was deeply influenced by Darwinian thought and the light that it might cast on the human mind. In fact, he believed that the study of evolution should be part of the education of every psychoanalyst (Ritvo, 1990; Kitcher, 1992). The disciplined application of Darwinian thought to psychology was not really possible during Freud's lifetime, largely because the genetic underpinnings of natural selection were not understood. Even after Mendelian genetics had been synthesized with evolutionary theory, it was only decades later when the work of George Williams and William Hamilton laid the groundwork for what is now popularly known as 'selfish gene' theory (Dawkins, 1976) that a true evolutionary psychology was possible. In 1975, Edmund O. Wilson published his monumental *Sociobiology*, which established a new field devoted to the study of the evolutionary basis of social behaviour (Wilson, 1975). A few years later, John Tooby and Leda Cosmides launched the discipline of evolutionary psychology. Wilson himself was primarily interested in the social behaviour of non-human animals, but other sociobiologists, and nearly all of the evolutionary psychologists, were deeply concerned with the light that the new discipline might throw on human beings.

Evolutionary theory holds that reproduction is the wellspring and motor of all life, including psychological life. Darwinian explanations of psychological phenomena ultimately involve specifying how a person's psychological tendencies subserved their reproductive interests in the prehistoric past. The Darwinian emphasis on reproduction sits very well with the centrality of sexual desire in the Freudian system. Furthermore, many of the topics investigated by sociobiologists and evolutionary psychologists, such as self-deception, sexuality and aggression, are also crucial to the Freudian conception of human nature. 'Darwinism's most significant contribution to psychology,' writes Symons (1987), 'may lie in its potential to shed light on these goals, wishes, purposes and desires – these mechanisms of feeling that motivate human action' (131).

Robert Trivers, one of the key figures in sociobiology, whose seminal work on parental investment, parent–offspring conflict, altruism, self-deception and the ramifications of sexual selection revolutionized our conception of how organisms, including human beings, interact with one another, was explicitly inspired by Freudian theory. Trivers was intrigued by research into the behaviour of rhesus monkeys, and used these observations to develop his theory of parent–offspring conflict. He recounts that in his biological research he was 'seeing that all the machinations Freud imagined going on early in life had reality' but which Freud had misunderstood (Bingham, 1980). In a 1985 interview published in *Omni* magazine, he expanded on the relationship of his work to that of Freud:

> I think Freud failed to establish a scientific methodology and tradition that would generate useful information for subsequent generations of psychologists. It's one of the scandals of modern psychoanalysis that more than seventy years have gone by and we still have so little scientifically usable information on key assumptions of the psychoanalytic system. I'd like to help lay the foundation that Freud failed to lay. (Trivers, 1985a)

From this perspective Freudian psychoanalysis and its derivatives appear to be precursors of sociobiology and evolutionary psychology. Psychoanalysis is thus reformed and extended by evolutionary thinking rather than being validated by it. It is only because of advances made in biology since the mid-1960s that these disciplines are now able to make good Freud's promissory note. Nesse and Lloyd (1992) make the connection between psychoanalysis and evolutionary psychology even more explicit:

> Freud's emphasis on the sexual origins of human motivation as reflected in the concept of 'libido' is remarkably congruent with the evolutionary psychobiologist's recognition of the crucial importance of reproductive success to human motivation. (619)

The apparent convergence between psychoanalytic and evolutionary thinking has given rise to a literature specifically aimed at using evolutionary thinking to garner support for psychoanalytic ideas (for example, Slavin and Kriegman, 1992; Badcock, 1994; Langs, 1996; Smith, 1999a), which contains a number of ideas about how evolutionary biology may cast new light on psychoanalytic theory and practice. Consider the example of parents' propensity to sacrifice their own interests for the benefit of their offspring. Hamilton (1964) demonstrated that when a parent 'selflessly' makes sacrifices for the benefit of her offspring, her behaviour increases the likelihood that her offspring will thrive and eventually reproduce, thereby proliferating her own genes. The mother's macroscopically altruistic actions are thus quite self-interested when viewed from the microscopic, genetic level. Hamilton's theory seems strongly consistent with Freud's (1914a) claim that parental love turns on adults projecting their own narcissism (self-love) onto their offspring. Like Hamilton, Freud claims that parental love is cryptically self-serving. So, are Freud and Hamilton saying much the same thing? Do psychoanalysis and evolutionary psychology share a common pattern of reasoning? Do they draw similar conclusions about the latent content of human behaviour?

Not necessarily. The philosopher David J. Buller has tackled this question in an important paper entitled 'De-Freuding Evolutionary Psychology' (Buller, 1999). Buller points out a critical distinction between evolutionary and Freudian explanation. According to psychoanalytic theory, self-serving, unconscious motives are disguised as socially acceptable conscious motives. Returning to the case of parental love, according to Freud's story, which is paradigmatic of the psychoanalytic explanatory style, a narcissistic psychological motive, the desire to adore and idealize oneself, is transformed into the adoration and idealization of one's children. In Hamilton's account, however, there is no latent self-serving psychological motive because gene-level selfishness, the *metaphorical* selfishness of the 'selfish gene', is not even a psychological state. Parental love is simply not a manifestation of repressed selfishness. Rather, Hamilton's theory states that parental love has been selected in to the repertoire of human behaviours because it enhances the proliferation of parental genes. Evolutionary explanations turn on the reproductive function of psychological phenomena, whereas psychoanalytic explanations consider their psychological functions. The convergence between psychoanalytic theory and evolutionary psychology may therefore be more apparent than real.

Although Buller's objection applies to evolutionary principles like Hamilton's rule, it does not apply equally well across the board, as there are other Darwinian accounts which describe evolved psychological structures and functions, just as psychoanalysis does. A prime example is Trivers' (1981) conception of the division of the mind into conscious and unconscious portions. Unlike the purely structural accounts of the unconscious provided by the majority of cognitive scientists, Trivers advances a dynamic conception of the mind in which motivated self-deception is fundamental. Briefly, Trivers argues that mental division is largely driven by interpersonal conflicts and their attendant affective concerns: human beings' propensity for deceit has been favoured by natural selection because individuals who are able to covertly exploit others have an advantage in the struggle for survival. By the same token, individuals with the ability to detect deception in a world full of deceivers, and who are therefore able protect themselves from exploitation, will have an adaptive advantage over their fellows. The evolution and proliferation of the propensity for deceit therefore encourages the evolution and proliferation of the ability to detect deception. According to Trivers, ever more sophisticated deceptive strategies were answered by ever more sensitive capacities for deception detection in an escalating evolutionary arms race. Intelligent deceivers are aware that there is risk of being discovered and are therefore burdened with anxiety. The stress generated by this situation is likely to be involuntarily expressed in bearing, voice and countenance. Trivers argues that the capacity for self-deception arose as a solution to this problem, for if one can deceive without being conscious of what one is doing, there is no cause for anxiety. By hiding the truth from ourselves we hide it more effectively from others. Our capacity for self-deception was greatly abetted by the evolution of language, which made it possible to lie, both to ourselves and to one another. According to Trivers (1981), the mind thus became split into two portions: an unconscious sector in possession of the truth, and a conscious portion closely linked to language and specialized at self-deception.

This *sounds* rather Freudian, but is it really? As was the case with the cognitive conception of the unconscious, Trivers' theory is consistent with psychoanalytic theory only on a very general level. Once we get down to specifics it is clear that the cracks are too large to paper over. Although it is true that both the Freudian theory of defence and Trivers' sociobiological theory of self-deception hold that the differentiation between the conscious and unconscious areas of the mind is driven by conflict, their accounts of this are wildly different. For Freudians, the repressed unconscious is formed as the result of conflicts between children and their parents, primarily concerning sexual wishes. The internalization of societal taboos, in the form of the superego, transmutes interpersonal conflicts into intrapsychic ones. Once the superego is established, the presence of forbidden sexual urges creates mental conflict and psychic pain, resulting in the banishment of the offending material from consciousness. In Trivers' theory there is no mention of childhood or infantile sexuality, and acts of self-deception are not instigated to protect the ego from mental pain. For Trivers, we deceive ourselves not to pre-empt inner distress, but to secure interpersonal advantages. Although more recent forms of psychoanalysis pay less attention to infantile sexuality as a motivating force, so far as I am aware, none of them coincides with the sociobiological story.

Psychotherapeutic outcome studies

Outcome studies examine the curative effects of psychoanalysis as a therapy. As I have already noted, even if psychoanalysis proved to be a uniquely effective form of psychotherapy, this would not mean that psychoanalytic theories have been proven true. Psychoanalysis might, as Freud (1916–17) mooted, be successful because it is a particularly clever form of cure through suggestion. By the same token, the failure of psychoanalysis to achieve better therapeutic results than its rivals or a credible placebo would not establish that psychoanalytic theories are false. After all, it is possible to know quite a bit about something without being able to use this knowledge as a basis for practical intervention: a science does not presuppose a corresponding 'technology'.

Outcome studies into psychoanalysis have been closely bound up with attempts to measure therapeutic outcome in psychotherapy generally. These efforts began in the 1950s and quickly led to a rather critical assessment of the curative claims of psychotherapists. The opening salvo was Hans Eysenck's paper 'The effects of psychother- apy: an evaluation' (1952) in which he argued that evidence suggests that although approximately two-thirds of patients seeking psycho- therapeutic help for neurotic problems are 'cured', this is also the rate of spontaneous remission in untreated neurotics. In other words, it looks like the patients who were allegedly helped by psychotherapy would have got better even if they had not been in treatment.

Attempts to empirically investigate outcomes in psychotherapy and psychoanalysis quickly became mired in methodological difficul- ties. One notorious example, the Menninger Clinic Project, took 18 years and a million dollars to generate results rendered completely invalid by the design flaws of the study (Rachman and Wilson, 1980). Attempts to measure the therapeutic effects of psychoanalysis are doubly problematic. Such efforts share the methodological problems inherent in psychotherapy research generally, but are also encum- bered with a set of difficulties that are specific to psychoanalysis.

Research into the effects of psychotherapy is notoriously difficult. Below are a small selection of the many difficulties described in the literature (Fonagy, no date; Kline, 1992; Roth and Fonagy, 1996).

1 *What is meant by 'recovery'?* Different forms of therapy have different definitions of what it means to be 'cured' of a psycho- logical disorder. If, say, behaviour therapists, Gestalt Therapists and psychoanalysts embrace radically different concepts of ther- apeutic success, how is it possible to find a common standard to compare their success rates?
2 *Personal characteristics of therapists.* It may be that certain psychotherapists obtain good or poor results, however these are to be identified, because of personal characteristics such as warmth and empathy. If this is the case, then measures of posi- tive outcome, however this is to be defined, may say more about the therapists involved in the study than they do about the method being tested.
3 *Interactional factors.* The outcome of therapy may be more determined by the 'chemistry' or fit between therapist and client than the specific modality being employed.
4 *Poor application.* A therapy that makes a poor showing in out- come studies may do so because the therapy has been badly or inappropriately applied, rather than because the therapeutic modality itself is ineffective.
5 *Questions of validity and reliability.* In order to measure psychological change one must possess an instrument to do the

measuring. The psychological test used must be both valid and reliable. A valid test is one that is adequately underwritten by empirical evidence. A reliable test is one that produces consistent results. Unfortunately, the psychological tests used to assess psychotherapy outcome are often dubious on both counts. 'Internal' validity is the way that the results of a study demonstrate the presence or absence of causal relations in the study itself. 'External' validity refers to what these results can tell us about phenomena in the wider world outside the study. Meaningful clinical research should display high levels of both internal and external validity; that is, a study should generate definite results that are applicable in the real world of clinical practice. Unfortunately, there is in practice an inverse relationship between internal and external validity in psychotherapy outcome studies. In order to be internally valid, the study must be tightly controlled, but this renders it unrepresentative of real clinical practice. 'The methodology that is truly adequate to the task of simultaneously assuring internal and external validity in psychotherapy research,' write Roth and Fonagy (1996: 20), 'has probably yet to be developed.'

6   *Variance effects.* It is possible that some psychotherapies may make some people much better and some much worse. In an outcome study, these effects may cancel one another out, so that the therapy *appears* to be having little or no effect.

According to Kline, the difficulties inherent in doing ideal psychotherapy research are so complex and profound that a study overcoming them would present enormous practical problems and demand vast resources (Kline, 1992). This means that in practice, psychotherapy researchers must cut corners, but in doing so the external validity of the study, the possibility of generalizing from it, becomes compromised. In the specific case of empirically testing psychoanalysis, these difficulties bite with a vengeance because the very nature of psychoanalytic therapy is such that it does not lend itself to the kind of regimentation required by standard outcome research protocols. Psychotherapy outcome studies are typically modelled on procedures for testing drugs (Stiles and Shapiro, 1994). The therapy is administered in a certain 'dosage' for a certain period of time and the effects, if any, are compared with the action of a placebo. The subjects receiving the treatment must be homogeneous, that is, they must all have the same 'illness'. They must also be randomly assigned to the treatment group and the control group that will receive the placebo, and they must be kept in the dark about which group they are in. This pharmacological model is grossly inappropriate for testing psychoanalysis. Psychoanalysts cannot and do not administer 'doses' of interpretation. Psychoanalysis is intricate and exploratory and involves lengthy periods of stasis, confusion and regression, which do not fit into neat formulations of a dose-response curve.

Many aspects of outcome research are actually antagonistic to the practice of psychoanalysis. For example, analysts place a high premium on privacy and confidentiality. It is believed that in order for an analysand to be completely free to discuss their darkest and most shameful secrets, the psychoanalytic setting must be completely protected from the eyes and ears of third parties. And yet, outcome research typically demands that third parties be involved in the treatment process, however indirectly. This very act of scrutiny may significantly disturb the process being studied. Outcome research is typically undertaken for therapy of a fixed duration, determined in advance by the experimenter, whereas psychoanalysis goes on until it is finished and cannot be squeezed into a procrustean timetable (Roth and Fonagy, 1996). Given that psychoanalysts describe the effects of psychoanalytic therapy as non-linear, that is, the client's psychological state may go through periods of apparent degeneration or stasis before ultimately improving, the use of fixed-duration therapy becomes especially problematic.

When researchers test the effects of psychotherapeutic approaches they often use *manualized* therapies. Manualizing a therapy means explicitly spelling out the rules for using its technique. This is important for psychotherapy outcome studies in order to ensure that all of the therapists in the sample are operating in the same way, just as when one is testing the effects of a new drug it is vital to ensure that all of the subjects receive the same dosage of an identical substance. It is no good attempting to draw conclusions about the effects of a form of psychotherapy if the practitioners generating the data are not practising in a reasonably uniform manner. This raises problems for testing psychoanalysis, which does not lend itself to this sort of regimentation. Even a single practitioner may practise psychoanalysis in variety of ways, depending on the nature of the client's problems, the chemistry between them and his or her stage of professional development; and different therapists belonging to the same school of psychoanalytic thought may conduct themselves in very different ways in their sessions. This is because the practice of psychoanalysis is often intuitive and idiosyncratic, relying more on analysts' assessments of their client's unconscious conflicts and intrapsychic structure than on particular 'techniques' deployed in well-circumscribed situations. It is arguable that psychoanalysis can no more be standardized than introspection which, if true, raises very deep problems for anyone wishing to empirically evaluate its outcomes.

In spite of these difficulties, there have been a considerable number of attempts to objectively evaluate the clinical potency of psycho-analysis (Bachrach et al., 1991; Crits-Christoph, 1992; Erwin, 1996; Fisher and Greenberg, 1996; Fonagy, no date; Lazar, 1997; Roth and Fonagy, 1996). Some of these studies have produced results that support psychoanalytic claims, while in others the results have been more negative. Irrespective of encouraging or dis-appointing outcomes, the fact remains that all of the studies hitherto undertaken have been so deeply bedevilled by methodological prob-lems that their results cannot be given a great deal of credence. The emotional intimacy of psychoanalysis, its extreme complexity, its ethical emphasis on the importance of privacy and confidentiality, and its sheer duration render it an unlikely target for empirical inves-tigation. These are essential features of psychoanalysis and cannot be minimized or eliminated without destroying the very organism that one is attempting to put under the microscope. Clinical psycho-analysis cannot reasonably be investigated by present-day methods, and may prove to be permanently refractory to controlled empirical investigation. As Edward Erwin (1996) tersely summed up after an exhaustive review of the research literature:

> We may not know that the therapy is generally ineffective ... but neither are we ever likely to be justified in believing that it is effective. The verdict ... that for any type of therapeutic benefit, there is no evi-dence that standard, long-term psychoanalysis is generally more effective in producing it than a credible, inexpensive placebo ... is likely to remain the final verdict. (292)

As it stands, we have no objective grounds for claiming either that psychoanalytic theory is largely true or that psychoanalytic methods really work. Although it is a powerful and evocative belief system and asks interesting and important questions about human beings, psycho-analysis seems to dangle in empirical limbo. In light of this disap-pointing and unsettling situation, we must now consider the question of whether it makes sense to approach psychoanalysis from an entirely different angle. Might it be that psychoanalysis is actually an inherently non-scientific but nonetheless a valid discipline? This 'hermeneutic' approach will be the subject of Chapter 4.

4
Hermeneutics in Focus

The preceding two chapters have concentrated on examining the scientific status and credibility of psychoanalysis, which has been found wanting. The cumulative critical efforts of philosophers of science and scientific investigators have precipitated an identity crisis for psychoanalysis. Its advocates have responded to this crisis in three ways. Many people strongly committed to psychoanalysis in theory and/or practice simply ignore the debate and the grave issues that it raises. A second, much smaller group agrees with the general thrust of the critical literature and has chosen to work at improving the scientific soundness of the discipline. Still others have met the challenge head on by asserting that scientific standards simply do not provide an appropriate yardstick for measuring psychoanalysis. According to this *hermeneutic* view, psychoanalysis is an interpretative discipline, more akin to literary criticism or perhaps historiography than to natural science, and as such owes its allegiance to a set of methodological and evidential norms that are quite distinct from the natural scientific ones.

The term 'hermeneutics' is derived from the Greek '*hermeneuein*' meaning 'to make something clear' (Thompson, 1996). Hermeneutics originated in the ancient world as a discipline for interpreting the meaning of the work of Classical Greek poets. Later, during the post-reformation Christian era, it was subsumed under theology and was used to establish the meaning of Biblical texts. Contemporary conceptions of hermeneutics are predominantly secular and largely based on the work of Schliermacher, Dilthey and Heidegger (Saks, 1999).

Before moving on to a detailed look at the hermeneutic approach to psychoanalysis, it is important to know what it is *not*. The hermeneutic psychoanalyst Donald Spence (1987) sets out the following five criteria that a discipline must satisfy in order to be counted as a member of the family of sciences:

1 Science is characterized by a respect for data, which is in the public domain and available to all interested parties.

2 Theories are driven by data; that is, they are consistent with evidence, responsive to new evidence, and modified or discarded in light of disconfirming data. Data is therefore given priority over beliefs or assumptions.
3 Science is cumulative. New advances extend and correct earlier views.
4 Argument is driven by logic and evidence rather than by authority. Science is thus 'fanatically democratic'.
5 Scientific theories are provisional and tentative, but are modified in response to new evidence rather than intellectual fashion.

Spence goes on to assert that, with respect to the five criteria, psychoanalysis fails on every count' (Spence, 1987: 74). It is easy to see why. Detailed descriptions of psychoanalytic data are quite rare. Data given in case studies is normally highly selective, and therefore suited for merely illustrative rather than evidential purposes. The ethical constraint of confidentiality also severely limits the degree to which clinical data can be made public, and a good deal of psycho-analytic 'data' consists of personal and subjective mental states which cannot even in principle enter the public domain. Also, as we have already seen, many if not most psychoanalytic theories are so extremely ambiguous and elastic that they cannot be refuted by inhospitable data. Psychoanalysis is thus primarily driven by theory rather than by data, and it is very rare for a psychoanalytic theory to be abandoned because of its empirical weaknesses. In spite of appearances, the trajectory of the development of psychoanalytic theory has not been cumulative. It might be said that psychoanalysis has not developed: it has just grown larger. Earlier views coexist with later ones, and texts written a century ago continue to be studied for their contemporary relevance. Of course, the advocates of any particular perspective will typically argue that their preferred theory is a decisive advance over earlier views, but these are subjective assessments with no bearing on the logic of development of the field as a whole. Psychoanalysis is notoriously authoritarian. Works by Freud, Klein, Jung and other psychoanalytic 'authorities' are not cited because of the data that they contain or the compelling inter-pretations of empirical data that they present. In fact, none of these authors present or consider data meeting even the most minimal scientific standards of adequacy. Psychoanalytic authorities are invoked purely because of the aura of credibility that they provide for the author. The authoritarian cast of psychoanalysis seems virtually inevitable in light of the fact that disputes cannot be resolved by appeals to data. After all, issues that cannot be resolved objectively and rationally will be dealt with through some other means.

Psychoanalysts often describe their theories and hypotheses as tentative. Indeed, ever since Bion (1970) introduced it to the analytic literature, it has been fashionable to invoke Keats' notion of 'negative capability' – the capacity to remain in doubt without grasping after certainty – as a description of the ideal psychoanalytic attitude. This vaunted attitude is, despite a superficial resemblance, worlds apart from the tentativeness of science. Scientific tentativeness is rooted in a critical attitude towards theories and a reluctance to make claims that are not fully warranted by the evidence at hand. Bionian negative capability does not even seek certainty. It idealizes uncertainty and, oddly, is often accompanied by the dogmatic attitude towards theoretical claims for which psychoanalysts of the Kleinian School have become notorious. Scientific theories are provisional because new evidence might, at any point, prove them wrong. Evidence (including the accumulation of anomalies) is the driving force behind scientific theory change. Because evidence is characteristically subordinated to theory in psychoanalysis, theory change is often more responsive to fashion than to data. There are many examples of sweeping theoretical changes in psychoanalysis, for example, the widespread and rapid proliferation of Kleinian, Lacanian and Kohutian ideas. I submit that Lacanism, to use what is perhaps the most dramatic example, has gained so many devoted adherents not because of the empirical virtues of Lacan's theories, but rather because of other, non-scientific attractions.

It may be, as the critics surveyed in Chapters 2 and 3 would have us believe, that these features of psychoanalysis are best explained by the idea that psychoanalysis is nothing but a pseudoscience, a science gone awry or a very poor attempt at science; but an alternative conclusion, promoted by the hermeneuticists, is that there is something fundamentally misconceived about the attempt to fit psychoanalysis to the Procrustean bed of natural science. Psychoanalysis will *inevitably* fail to measure up to scientific standards, they say, because its subject matter – human subjectivity – cannot possibly be captured by the kind of methodological net employed by physicists and biologists. They argue that the study of human subjectivity is an interpretative discipline rather than a natural science, and is concerned with the meanings that human subjects give to their own experiences rather than the causal underpinnings of those experiences. Freud's conviction that his brainchild was a natural science, and his belief that the human mind could and should be studied like any other natural thing, is of merely historical significance and does not, according to the hermeneuticists, have any substantive bearing on their arguments. Freud, it is said, suffered from a scientistic self-misunderstanding (Habermas, 1971), and thus misconstrued his own undertaking. Hermeneutic renditions of psychoanalysis attempt to strip away the inappropriate accretions of scientific thinking that adhere to psychoanalysis in consequence of Freud's grave error.

There are at least five varieties of hermeneutic psychoanalysis. Although all of these have certain themes in common, there are also significant differences between them. In the present chapter I will limit myself to examining major and characteristically hermeneutic themes without devoting attention to the fine differences between particular versions of hermeneutic psychoanalysis. For the latter, the reader can do no better than to consult Elyn Saks's *Interpreting Interpretation: The Limits of Hermeneutic Psychoanalysis* (Saks, 1999).

Meaning and causation

One of the most central and persistent themes in the hermeneutic literature is the distinction between meaning and causation. Psychoanalysis, it is said, should be concerned with the domain of meaning: the meaning of symptoms, dreams, parapraxes and other products of the unconscious mind. Although Freud was devoted to the discovery of meaning, his natural-scientific bias led him to confuse the search for meanings, reasons, motives or intentions with the search for the causes of behaviour.

The notion that Freud confused meanings (or reasons) with causes was given considerable impetus by Ludwig Wittgenstein's lectures at Cambridge University in the early part of the twentieth century. Wittgenstein argued that explanations invoking causes are validated in an entirely different manner than explanations invoking reasons, and that Freud misguidedly used the two interchangeably. 'I see,' he remarked, 'a muddle here between a cause and a reason.' (Wittgenstein, 1982: 10). Wittgenstein claimed that the difference between reasons and causes is brought out by the fact that the investigation of a cause is carried out experimentally, whereas the investigation of a reason 'entails as an essential part one's agreement with it' (ibid.). That psychoanalysis concerns itself with reasons rather than causes is shown, according to Wittgenstein, by the patient's ultimate epistemic authority: we only know for sure that an interpretation is correct when the patient assents to it. There is nothing in the scientific investigation of causes that remotely resembles this validating procedure.

Wittgenstein's analysis and related hermeneutic arguments turning on the dichotomy between meanings and causes are problematic on two counts. First, Wittgenstein's story is an inaccurate exegesis of Freudian thinking on the validation of interpretations. Psychoanalysts do not and should not regard an interpretation as confirmed only or especially when a patient consciously agrees with it. Freud (for example, 1937) was quite explicit that conscious assent is neither a necessary nor a sufficient condition for regarding an interpretation as correct, just as conscious dissent does not mean that an interpretation is wrong, for agreement with an interpretation can be an expression of positive transference and rejecting it an expression of resistance. Considering the issue more deeply, it is obvious that relying on conscious assent would be inconsistent with the basic psychoanalytic conception of the structure and operation of the mind. The conscious mind of the analytic patient is just as much an 'outsider' to his or her unconscious mind as the analyst is. We do not have privileged access to the contents of our unconscious minds and we are therefore in no position to validate or refute a psychoanalytic interpretation on introspective grounds. Although the issue of just how interpretations are to be validated remains controversial, there is a broad consensus that they are to be evaluated on the basis of their *effects* (Freud, 1937; Kernberg, 1994; Langs, 1982a).

The second, and more fundamental, problem with Wittgenstein's hermeneutic argument lies in the very idea of a radical dichotomy between reasons and causes. This distinction was taken virtually as gospel in the world of philosophy until the groundbreaking work of the American philosopher Donald Davidson in the early 1970s, which demonstrated that reasons are themselves a type of cause (Davidson, 1970). When we consider the definition of a cause as any event that makes a difference to the occurrence of some other event, Davidson's insight becomes screamingly obvious. There can be no doubt, for example, that Winston's thirst conjoined with his belief that drinking a beverage will quench his thirst act together to bring about his pouring himself a glass of beverage. Furthermore, it is not true that assent is the *sine qua non* for validating a hypothesis about someone's reason for doing something. We come to conclusions about motives largely on the basis of our understanding of human nature, and these considerations often override the weight we place on what individuals say about the meaning of their actions (particularly when these motives involve feelings of shame or guilt, as is paradigmatically the case in psychoanalysis). So, even in the case of conscious motives, assent is not always an appropriate touchstone for validation. It seems that Freud's mingling causal with intentional vocabularies was not a 'muddle' after all: motives do cause actions, and unconscious motives cannot, by their very nature, be validated by conscious assent.

The other reason why Wittgenstein's story fails as a reinterpretation of Freud concerns his use of a standard philosophical account of reasons, which holds that reasons are combinations of desires and beliefs. Desires specify ends, and beliefs specify means. So, for example, if Elaine desires to be a millionaire and believes that buying a lottery ticket will cause her to become a millionaire, this desire/belief pair provide the reason for her buying a lottery ticket. There is a clear logical relationship between desires, beliefs and the resultant actions. This is true even if the desires and beliefs involved are very strange. If Reinfeld desires to be immortal and he believes that eating spiders will make him immortal he will, all things being equal, dine on spiders as frequently as possible. Although it is very strange to eat spiders, Reinfeld's actions are rational in the sense that they follow logically from his premises. According to Freud's theory, unconscious motives do not have anything like a logical structure. For example, he writes in *The Ego and the Id* (1923a) that:

> We approach the id with analogies: we call it a chaos, a cauldron full of seething excitations. ... It is filled with energy reaching it from the instincts, but it has no organization, produces no collective will, but only a striving to bring about the satisfaction of the instinctual needs. (73)

Psychoanalytic clinical formulations are, on the whole, consistent with Freud's conception of the essential irrationality of the unconscious. For example, Freud (1901) recounts how the Austrian prime minister, facing a hostile parliament, opened parliament with the words 'I now declare parliament *closed*'. If we assume that the unconscious conforms to the practical syllogism, that is, the rational formula that desire/belief pairs provide the reasons for actions, Freud would be committed to something like the following explanation of the parapraxis:

1 The Prime Minister did not want to open parliament.
2 He unconsciously believed that by substituting the word 'closed' for the word 'open' he would prevent parliament from being opened.
3 Therefore he said 'I now declare parliament closed'.

The obvious problem with this reconstruction lies in step two, which seems neither intuitively plausible nor consistent with what Freud and other psychoanalysts have to say about the way that unconscious processes actually work. Psychoanalysts regard slips as ... slips! They are unintentional acts caused by the non-rational impact of suppressed thoughts. Slips are not even unconsciously calculated: they are simply the outcome of mental conflict. A further difficulty raised by the insistence that psychoanalysis should confine itself to the language of agency lies in the implications of this constraint for the psychoanalytic concept of psychical determinism. The theory of psychical determinism or 'the determination of mental life' asserts that the human mind is subject to casual laws in much the same way as the rest of the universe. The principle of psychical determinism is incompatible with metaphysical ideas of free will and radical human autonomy. 'Psychoanalysts,' writes Freud, 'are marked by a particularly strict belief in the determinism of mental life. For them there is nothing trivial, nothing arbitrary or haphazard. They expect in every case to find sufficient motives where, as a rule, no such expectation is raised' (Freud, 1910a: 38). 'All mental events,' he claims, 'are completely determined' (1920: 64). This is made vividly clear in almost any clinical psychoanalytic text, as well as works on dreams and parapraxes. For example, Freud asserted in *The Psychopathology of Everyday Life* (1901) that it is impossible to think of a name at random. On one occasion a patient challenged this view, and Freud suggested that they perform an experiment on the spot. Freud asked him to think of a woman's name. As the young man was quite promiscuous, a large number of women's names might have come readily to mind. The first name that came to the man's mind was 'Albine' (pronounced in German as '*Albina*'), which was strange because he did not actually know anyone named Albine. However, Freud remarks, the young man had a very fair complexion (Freud sometimes jokingly called him 'albino') and the man's analysis was at the time primarily concerned with the feminine side of his nature, 'So it was he himself who was this "Albine", the woman who was the most interesting to him at the moment' (108). The issue here is not the correctness of Freud's conclusions, which the reader may or may not find compelling, but rather his pattern of reasoning: the name 'Albine' *intruded* into the man's mind in response to inner psychological pressures rather than as the end-product of an intentionalistic, rational sequence of thoughts.

Psychology versus metapsychology

Freud's allegedly misguided preoccupation with causation was embodied in the body of abstract theory in psychoanalysis known as 'metapsychology'. Metapsychology describes the mind or 'mental apparatus' in purely subpersonal and physicalistic terms, referring to mental forces, the discharge of energy, and mental systems or locations and makes no reference whatsoever to human agency, subjectivity or meaning. When psychoanalysts talk about regions of the mind (conscious, preconscious, unconscious), mental agencies (id, ego, superego), drives (aggression, sexuality, narcissism) and so on, they are engaging in metapsychological discourse. Many hermeneutic thinkers have called for the expurgation of metapsychology from psychoanalysis (for example, Klein, 1976; Schafer, 1976; Strenger, 1991).

Freud's creation of metapsychology was a vital ingredient of his larger programme of constructing a comprehensive science of the mind. A crucial aspect of this ambitious project was the integration of psychology with neuroscience. Freud attempted in 1895 to create just such an integrative neuropsychology in his *Project for a Scientific Psychology* (Freud, 1950) which he soon abandoned not, as some would have it, because he came to believe that psychology should have no truck with neuroscience (Schwartz, 1999), but rather because he did not believe that an integrated psycho-neuroscientific model of the mind was possible during his lifetime, probably because neuroscience was not yet a sufficiently mature science. Freud never abandoned the hope that scientists of future generations might reduce his psychological theories to neuroscientific principles (Smith, 1999a; 2000) and his metapsychology was an attempt to cast the fundamental theories of psychoanalysis in a form that would be hospitable to neuroscientific reduction. 'Metapsychology' literally means 'beyond psychology': it was Freud's attempt to move beyond purely psychological descriptions to the neurophysiological level which he believed to lie behind them. He therefore spoke of the movement of 'energy' within and between functional systems, of processes of charge and discharge, of psychical 'locations' and so on. Although Freudian metapsychology is more attuned to the neuroscience of the late nineteenth century than it is to present-day views, and a case can easily be made for discarding much of it as it stands, the hermeneutic rejection of metapsychology *per se* is tantamount to rejecting Freud's central intellectual ambition for psychoanalysis.

Hermeneutic psychoanalysts characteristically view psychoanalysis as a method of investigating human subjectivity. Of course, there is a trivial sense in which this is and must be true by virtue of the fact that psychoanalysis investigates human subjects. Medical science too is concerned with human subjects, yet it would be absurd to consider medicine a science of subjectivity. The sense in which 'subjectivity' is used here is perhaps best captured by Buller's (1999) distinction between personal and sub-personal explanation. The hermeneuts regard the level of personhood as explanatory bedrock: for them, the task of psychoanalysis is to understand how human agents deal with conflicting desires, emotions, goals and feelings. Sub-personal explanations in terms of drives and neurophysiological processes are not regarded as having a legitimate place underneath the psychoanalytic umbrella. Although he did not define himself as a hermeneut, one of the prominent expositors of this position was the American analyst Heinz Kohut, who asserted in his influential 1959 paper on *Introspection, empathy and psychoanalysis* (Kohut, 1959) that introspection and vicarious introspection (empathy) are the only legitimate tools for psychoanalytic research; psychoanalysis is thus essentially the study of the patient's felt, and therefore conscious, experience. For Kohut, even theoretical entities such as drives are, in the final analysis, mere abstractions from felt, introspective experience of states possessing the quality of 'drivenness'. Kohut's derivation of the drives is logically similar to Wittgenstein's critique of what he took to be the derivation of the concept of the unconscious in psychoanalysis. According to Wittgenstein, analysts speak of the unconscious when they are unaware of the cause of a mental event, feeling or piece of behaviour. 'The unconscious' is therefore nothing more than a grammatical gimmick serving as a cover-up for ignorance. 'We might,' argues Wittgenstein, 'imagine a language in which one does not say "We do not know who did that," but "Mr Donotknow did that" – so as not to have to say that one does not know something' (Wittgenstein, 1976: 402). As Bouveresse (1995: 34) remarks in his commentary on Wittgenstein, 'To say that the unconscious did this or that … is first of all what allows us to avoid saying that we do not know who (or what) has done this.' In other words, although one might act unconscious*ly*, that is, without a true understanding of one's own motives, there is no such thing as *the* unconscious.

The hermeneutic psychoanalyst Roy Schafer used Wittgensteinian reasoning to purge psychoanalysis of all metapsychological language, replacing it with his own hermeneutically-inspired 'action language'. Schafer laid out his plan for purification in the 1976 book *A New Language for Psychoanalysis* (Schafer, 1976), where he described metapsychology as a language rather than a collection of models or theories. Metapsychology is a deeply misleading language because it describes human beings mechanistically as objects propelled by forces, thus violating the fundamental hermeneutic principle that human beings are properly understood as agents inspired by motives. According to Schafer, the psychoanalytic unconscious properly refers both to the way that human beings misrepresent their own actions to themselves in order to avoid anxiety, guilt, shame or other forms of emotional discomfort, and also to 'would-be' actions: those actions which one wishes to perform but refrains from performing. If we follow Schafer, there is no philosophically suspect mysterious unconscious domain. Unconsciousness is adverbial: it is a quality of some forms of human agency.

The problem haunting all such attempts to dispose of metapsychology is the restriction of psychological explanation to the language of human agency. Is a newborn baby an agent? If not, when and how does a baby become an agent? Is a dreamer an agent? Are obsessions, phobias, hallucinations and other symptoms of mental disorders expressions of human agency? Is human biology utterly detached from and impotent to influence the psyche? The rejection of the kind of causal and biological thinking that inspired metapsychology implies the view that the human mind somehow stands outside of the material universe. This is a philosophically retrograde position, more characteristic of seventeenth and eighteenth century thought than the philosophy and science of today. It is also quite antagonistic to the radically naturalistic spirit that inspired the creation of psychoanalysis, Freud's view that 'the intellect and the mind are objects for scientific research in exactly the way of any non-human things' (Freud, 1933: 159).

The problem of conflicting intuitions

In common with other hermeneutic defenders of psychoanalysis, the philosopher Charles Taylor denies that science is the only valid way of knowing about the world. Taylor (1985) argues that if this were the case, then the kinds of inference that we routinely make in everyday life would be invalidated. When we say that Jamaica is a lovely country, that Miss Ann has a terrific sense of humour, or that Marcia is a warm person, we are not dealing with the kinds of things that can be scientifically regimented and subjected to the rules governing empirical inferences. In short, we do not and cannot restrict our lives to scientifically validated principles. According to Taylor (1979) psychoanalytic interpretations, like the judgements we make in everyday life, are based on intuitive credibility. The philosophical use of the term 'intuition' is different than its use in everyday language. In philosophical discourse, intuition means immediate, non-inferential knowledge. For a proposition to be intuitively credible, then, is for it to 'feel right'. According to Taylor, psychoanalytic interpretations are to be judged on the basis of their intuitive resonance rather than the natural science standards surveyed in preceding chapters. An obvious objection to Taylor's thesis comes from psychoanalysis itself. As Freud was fond of pointing out, many psychoanalytic interpretations are, by commonsensical standards, deeply *counter*intuitive. Furthermore, psychoanalytic propositions are often rejected because of the emotional resistances that they evoke. How can these non-scientifically based rejections of psychoanalysis be squared with Taylor's claim that psychoanalysis is underwritten by intuition? The standard psychoanalytic approach to this problem is that psycho-analytic claims are credible only to a purified intuition. It is only when the irrational resistances to psychoanalytic truth have been cleared away, normally by means of psychoanalytic treatment, that psycho-analytic propositions are recognized as self-evidently true. Taylor seems to argue for something like this, stating that in the hermeneu-tic 'sciences of man' (of which psychoanalysis is an example) it is legitimate to ask the critic to change himself.

Is this a reasonable recommendation? In cases of intuitive dis-agreement, it is not clear which of the two parties should change themselves (Erwin, 1996). Lorraine, a committed Freudian, finds Freud's interpretation of Dora's cough as expressing a repressed fel-latio fantasy deeply compelling, whereas Vinetta, a sceptic, regards it as preposterous. Who should change themselves, Lorraine, Vinetta or both? It is unavailing to say that the person who is wrong should change, for as Erwin (1996) points out, intuition alone cannot tell us which of them is wrong. This problem with Taylor's argument is one of the major drawbacks of all of the hermeneutic approaches. Once objectivity is discarded and intuition lionized, we are left with no rational method for adjudicating between rival intuitions. The hermeneut cannot coherently suggest that the view best supported by evidence should win the day, because the epistemic value of objective evidence has already been discarded in favour of subjective intuition. As we will see, this problem opens the door to the view that there is no such thing as psychoanalytic truth, and that the best that psychoanalysis can do is to create stories about the human condition.

Truth and the ethics of hermeneutic psychoanalysis

In many, if not most, versions of hermeneutic psychoanalysis, the concern with the truth of an interpretation has been replaced by a concern with its pragmatic virtues. It is easy to see the reason for this shift, particularly in the light of the preceding discussions of the epistemological liabilities of psychoanalytic reasoning as diagnosed by philosophers such as Nagel, Popper and especially Grünbaum. Perhaps the renewed emphasis on the use of pragmatic yardsticks to judge interpretations is motivated by a desire to sidestep the deep epistemological problems that philosophers of science have brought to light.

If we claim, as Freud did, that psychoanalytic theory provides a true account of the operation of the human psyche, that good interpretations offer true pictures of people's unconscious mental life and that interpretations have positive psychotherapeutic consequences precisely because of their truth, we are saddled with the onerous problem of finding some independent method for evaluating these claims. Psychoanalytic interpretations, and the theories from which they are in part deduced, are classically causal propositions. When, for example, an analyst offers an interpretation of a dream, he or she offers a causal hypothesis of the form 'You may have had the following dream *because* of the activation of unconscious wish X'. As both philosophers of science and hermeneutic thinkers have pointed out, causal claims are best assessed inductively by means of either natural or contrived experiments, whereas psychoanalytic interpretations are never given this kind of treatment. Philosophers like Grünbaum conclude that psychoanalysis will never be intellectually credible until it lives up to natural-scientific standards of epistemic justification, whereas the hermeneutic psychoanalytic apologists respond that, as a 'human' science, psychoanalysis should be free to apply its own standards of justification and not be enslaved by the natural-scientific model.

One widespread belief about how this might work in practice is to abandon the conventional scientific account of 'truth' entirely (Spence, 1982; Steele, 1979; Viderman, 1979). Scientists typically make use of what is called the 'correspondence theory' of truth, according to which a statement is true if and only if it matches how the world really is. For instance, the statement 'snow is white' is true if, and only if, snow really is white. Freud was committed to the correspondence theory of truth. In fact, his Tally Argument, which states that an interpretation is curative if and only if it 'tallies' with what is real in the patient, is a correspondence-based account. Many hermeneuts distance themselves from this approach, claiming that psychoanalysts should not concern themselves with truth, in the classical sense, at all. For them, interpretations are not propositions that may be true or false, they are stories which patients may find therapeutically useful or useless. A 'good' interpretation is therefore not by definition true, as Freud would have it: psychoanalytic interpretation is more like the 'interpretation' of a Beethoven sonata (Steele, 1979) or of a literary work: neither true nor false, although more or less moving and meaningful. Similarly, a single sonata can be 'interpreted' in a number of ways, all equally valid, and there is no single 'true' interpretation.

How can interpretations, construed in this way, have curative effects? It may be that psychoanalysis works by altering the stories that people tell themselves about their own lives. As a result of therapy, limited, destructive, frustrating or self-defeating narratives may be abandoned and replaced by more hopeful, dynamic and liberating ones. Additionally, psychoanalysis may provide patients with stories where previously they had none, smoothing over the chaotic rough edges of a fragmented life. 'Meaningful stories,' writes Saks (1999), 'can be therapeutic inasmuch as uncertainty – still more, confusion – is psychologically debilitating. When the pieces of the puzzle fit together one feels comforted. A gain in meaning, then, is a gain in well-being.' (85). Donald Spence (1982), one of the most prominent and articulate representatives of the hermeneutic trend, writes that:

> The linguistic and narrative aspects of an interpretation may well have priority over its historical truth, and we are making the somewhat heretical claim that an interpretation is effective because it gives the awkward happening a kind of linguistic and narrative closure, not because it can account for it in a purely causal sense. An interpretation satisfies because we are able to contain an unfinished piece of reality in a meaningful sentence. ... The power of language is such that simply putting something into words gives it a certain kind of authenticity ... . (138)

The hermeneutic approach is an attractive option to defenders of psychoanalysis for two broad reasons. As we have seen, it mobilizes a defence against critics who slate psychoanalysis as unscientific by providing a considered alternative to the natural-scientific model, although at the cost of rejecting the way that Freud and nearly all of the classical writers on psychoanalysis conceived of the discipline. By rejecting the idea that interpretations should be true, in the conventional scientific sense, hermeneutic writers undercut the charge that psychoanalysts are unable to underwrite their hollow truth claims with hard evidence.

The second attraction relates to an embarrassing feature of contemporary psychoanalysis to which I have not yet given emphasis. Psychoanalysis is, and has been for some time, extremely diverse. As I have already noted, there are numerous schools of thought and practice even within the psychoanalytic mainstream, not to mention its fringes. The proliferation of psychoanalytic schools means that there is very little clinical and theoretical consensus. Psychoanalysts of all stripes tend to regard their theories and interpretations as basically true depictions of mental life, but unfortunately many if not most of these approaches are mutually incompatible. In other words, from the standpoint of any one committed practitioner, representatives of rival schools must be mistaken. To make matters worse, there is not even consensus within any given 'school'. The comparative literature shows that competent Freudians are likely to reach very different conclusions about the interpretation of a given case. The same is true of Jungians, Kleinians, and so on. How can this high level of diversity be squared with the idea that psychoanalysts possess a true understanding of the psyche? According to the hermeneutic writers, it can't and it needn't be. Psychoanalytic diversity provides narrative variety. All of these approaches are equally valid and effective because each weaves powerful and effective stories for patients to apply to their lives. From a trainee's point of view, the decision to train in one approach or another becomes less agonizing. It is no longer necessary to decide which approach is objectively 'best'. The question of choosing a training becomes an aesthetic question, like choosing the colour of the bedroom wallpaper: what kind of therapeutic narrative resonates most profoundly with my personality?

There are several problems with this proposal. First, it is questionable whether the whole history of psychoanalysis can be reinterpreted along hermeneutic lines without trivializing it. The quest for causal explanations for dreams, slips and symptoms and the commitment to creating a comprehensive scientific theory of the mind were not just minor, incidental features of the psychoanalytic research programme as conceived of by Freud and the early analysts. These features were central to what these men and women were attempting to achieve. Given that the hermeneutic analysts surgically remove the heart of Freud's psychoanalysis, replacing it with an attitude towards truth that he and his colleagues would have felt to be deeply repugnant, it may be somewhat disingenuous to call the resulting discipline 'psychoanalysis'. Furthermore, the goals of hermeneutic analysis as a therapy seem to be quite different from those of classical psychoanalytic therapy. Classical psychoanalysis aimed to eliminate patients' neurotic symptoms rather than make them less distressed. As Freud famously put it in the *Studies on Hysteria* (Freud and Breuer, 1895), the aim of psychoanalysis is to replace neurotic suffering with ordinary unhappiness. It is not clear how a mere story, no matter how meaningful, compelling and coherence-promoting, can eliminate a psychological symptom unless this is due to a suggestive placebo effect. But this is surely not what the hermeneuts have in mind, for the revelation that psychoanalysis works because of its placebo effects would be cold comfort to practitioners. So, whatever its virtues, the hermeneutic approach is so fundamentally at odds with the classical psychoanalytic approaches on a deep philosophical level that perhaps it should not be called psychoanalysis at all.

Second, is it really true that the hermeneutic 'take' on psychoanalysis manages to evade the need for scientific justification? Hermeneutic writers claim that it is the *coherence* brought about by an interpretation, rather than its truth-value, that carries a therapeutic effect. But this itself is a causal claim. To say, as Spence does, that the 'semantic closure' brought about by an interpretation relieves psychological distress is just to say that these properties of the interpretation *cause* the amelioration of distress (there is no real difference between 'bringing about' an event and 'causing' it). Given that causal claims, as many hermeneutic writers admit, are properly assessed through the empirical methods of natural science, it follows that the hermeneutic approach is beholden to the very standards that it has rejected! The same is true of the problem of therapeutic effects mentioned above. Does hermeneutic psychoanalysis have therapeutic effects only because of its suggestive power? There is no way of investigating this important question without recourse to the despised methodology of natural science. It seems that even the hermeneutic approach cannot escape the need for scientific scrutiny.

The third problem is an ethical one, identified by Elyn Saks (1999). Saks considers the hermeneutic approach from the patient's point of view. She argues that patients will and should reject 'a version of psychoanalysis that holds out to them stories that do not purport to be possibly true' (121). Patients who enter the momentous, expensive and time-consuming process of psychoanalysis do not want to be fobbed off with mere stories. Unless analysts' stories at least purport to be true, an analytic patient has no rational basis for believing them, and unless he or she actually believes in the stories it is difficult to understand how they could possibly have the reassuring effect touted by proponents of the hermeneutic approach. Of course, one option open to analysts is to lie to patients about what they are doing. An analyst may believe that his or her interpretations are only stories, but conceal this belief from patients who are implicitly led to believe that the interpretations given by the analyst are at least purportedly true. Indeed, it is difficult to imagine why any person would enter into therapy with a hermeneutic psychoanalyst unless this sort of deception was in place. Imagine an analyst who cheerfully informs prospective patients that 'I am going to tell you stories about yourself and your past which I do not believe to be true but, hey, this doesn't really matter as long as *you* believe them.' Would any sane person willingly entrust themselves to such a person? Should they? Yet to lie about it would be an unethical breach of trust calling into question the fundamental integrity of the psychoanalytic relationship.

Conclusion

Although superficially attractive as a radical refutation of criticisms levelled against the scientific credibility of psychoanalysis, the hermeneutic option is so riddled with philosophical, conceptual and ethical problems that it is unable to provide a viable alternative.

1 Despite hermeneutic claims to the contrary, reasons and causes cannot be radically separated. Reason-explanations are a kind of causal explanation.
2 Although many hermeneutic psychoanalysts wish to explain mental phenomena as the result of latent reasons, paradigmatically psychoanalytic explanations of dreams, slips, symptoms and the like invoke mental causes which are not reasons.
3 In rejecting metapsychology, hermeneutic psychoanalysts reject the fundamental integrative scientific vision of psychoanalysis.
4 If the truth of psychoanalytic interpretations is evaluated purely intuitively, what happens when intuitions conflict? The hermeneutic approach has no objective means for adjudicating between rival intuitions.
5 If the very concept of 'truth' is expunged from psychoanalysis, and interpretations are said to work not because of their truth but because of their organizing effects, how is this *causal* claim

to be evaluated without reverting to natural-scientific norms and methods? The hermeneutic approach has no cogent answer to this.

6 The hermeneutic approach rejects so much that was philosophically basic to classical psychoanalysis that it may be illegitimate for it to be considered as a form of psychoanalysis.

7 Patients will not and should not entrust their psyches to an analyst who claims to do nothing more than tell them stories about themselves which do not even purport to be true, and it is unethical for analysts to conceal from patients that this is what they are doing.

The hermeneutic approach provides no reassurance for psychoanalysis, as it is vulnerable on both epistemological and ethical grounds. It is now time to turn away from this abstract and philosophical level of analysis and focus our attention on what is perhaps one of the strongest and most central of specific psychoanalytic concepts: the unconscious.

5
The Unconscious and Free Association in Focus

Freud's specific proposals about the nature of unconscious mental activity form the cornerstone of psychoanalytic theory. The idea of the unconscious was controversial during much of Freud's lifetime, and remains controversial in many quarters today. In this chapter I will first give something of the history of the concept of the unconscious and then quickly dispose of a few very naive criticisms that are nonetheless frequently invoked by psychotherapists. I will then go on to draw on some more sophisticated and substantial criticisms of the concept of unconscious mental activity and demonstrate some of their weaknesses using Freud's own strategies. Finally, I will critically examine the free association method, which is the primary psychoanalytic tool for accessing unconscious mental states.

Historical background

The concept of the unconscious grew out of the failure of the orthodox psychology of consciousness to successfully confront challenges posed by scientific developments in the mid- to late-nineteenth century. The orthodox view had its roots in the writings of the seventeenth century French philosopher and polymath René Descartes who proposed that the mind is entirely conscious, and that one simply cannot be mistaken about the contents of one's own mind. This general conception of the mind was very widely accepted by psychologists, neuroscientists and philosophers during the nineteenth and early twentieth centuries. In the early years of his career, Freud too unswervingly accepted the traditional view. However, as he gained experience as a clinician and was confronted with the task of making theoretical sense of his observations, he abandoned it. From 1895 onwards Freud held that mental processes are fundamentally unconscious.

Freud set out his new model in *The Interpretation of Dreams* (1900), where the human mind is depicted as composed of three systems: System Unconscious (*Ucs.*), System Preconscious (*Pcs.*) and

System Conscious (*Cs.*). System Unconscious, or 'the unconscious', consists of thoughts that have no access to consciousness. Preconscious contents, on the other hand, are thoughts that are only *temporarily* unconscious: they are poised to become conscious. In order for a mental content to move from *Ucs.* to *Pcs.* it must pass across a barrier that Freud called the 'censorship'. The censor excludes or 'represses' those thoughts that would produce intense guilt or shame if they were to become conscious. This model in effect represents the mind as analogous to an electronic computer. System Unconscious is rather like the processing unit, where all the work takes place, whereas consciousness resembles the monitor, which merely displays information generated by the processing unit. The censorship is rather like a filter controlling the flow of information between the processor and the monitor determining just what information is to be displayed on the screen of awareness.

In 1923 Freud published *The Ego and The Id*, where he completely discarded the division of the mind into *Ucs, Pcs.* and *Cs.* From this point onwards he understood unconsciousness as a *property* rather than as a mental module, a modifier rather than a noun. Freud no longer spoke of *the* unconscious, or *System Ucs.* and instead spoke of unconscious memories, unconscious fantasies, unconscious ideas and so on.

Some naive objections

There is a large literature dealing with the validity of the concept of the unconscious in both its psychoanalytic and non-psychoanalytic forms. It is also a very uneven literature, where naive and fallacious arguments rub shoulders with incisive philosophical and scientific discussions. I will first clear away some of the naive and poorly argued objections to the unconscious which, in spite of their flimsy nature, are widely stated and re-stated in the psychotherapeutic literature. Many of these are based on crude misunderstandings of psychoanalytic theory, or on antiquated or misguided philosophical conceptions of the mind. Having done this, I will move on to consider several more thoughtful objections.

1 Sartre's objection

Jean-Paul Sartre set out one of the most popular naive objections to the concept of the unconscious in his monumental tome *Being and Nothingness* (1956). Sartre argued that because the Freudian censorship (which he falsely believes to demarcate consciousness from the unconscious) must be aware of the mental contents that it excludes from consciousness, it follows that the censor must be conscious of them, and if the censor is conscious of them, then we cannot say that the subject is actually unconscious of so-called repressed ideas. This is really a very silly argument that has for some mysterious reason been so influential that it has generated a literature of its own (Cannon, 1991; Gardner, 1993; Smith, 1994, 1995; Spinelli, 1993, 1994). The obvious defect in Sartre's reasoning is his implicit claim that perceiving something means being conscious of it. There is no logically compelling reason for this assumption. In fact, if it were the case, then the search engine on my computer would arguably have to be conscious of the Web sites that it selects for me when I am surfing the Web. Sartre's error stems from his unquestioning commitment to the Cartesian doctrine of the translucency of consciousness, the dogmatic and axiomatic assumption that consciousness equates to mind. Advocates of Sartre's view typically replace the binary distinction between conscious and unconscious states with the allegedly superior notion of gradations in consciousness: some mental states are said to be less conscious than others, but all are nevertheless regarded as levels of consciousness. The notion of gradations in consciousness is sometimes used as a refutation of the binary conscious/unconscious distinction. The idea here is that if there are degrees of consciousness, and one can therefore be either more or less conscious of some item at any given time, it follows that so-called unconscious awareness is not really *unconscious*: it is actually a dimly conscious state. In fact, this does not follow at all. The argument is like claiming that because there are big fish, smaller fish and still smaller fish there is no such thing as a nonfish. It is certainly arguable that there are gradations in consciousness, but, as Freud himself recognized (see below), this conception is perfectly compatible with the claim that there are also radically unconscious states.

2 If you can't see it, it isn't real

A second naive objection is that the unconscious is unobservable, and should therefore be disregarded or at the very least treated in a highly circumspect fashion. The idea that unobservable entities are somehow suspect and should be dispensed with was popular with the logical positivists in the early decades of the twentieth century, but is no longer regarded as a tenable position. Contemporary science *depends* on postulating the existence of unobservable entities. Quantum physics, which is probably the most successful scientific theory ever, is to a very great extent a science of unobservable entities, as was the science of genetics until very recently. The person who would dispense with the unconscious on the grounds of unobservability would also reject quantum mechanics, stop genetics dead in its tracks, and illegitimize vast swathes of science. A variation of this criticism is the claim that because unconscious items are unobservable, talk about them readily leads to dogmatism and superstition. Although this objection perhaps unwittingly concedes the existence of unconscious mental events, and therefore is not an objection to the notion of the unconscious *per se*, it gives an extremely implausible account of the relationship between the use of theoretical entities and the disposition to dogmatism. As the example of quantum physics demonstrates, the use of theoretical entities does not in itself generate dogmatism and superstition. Of course, some advocates of the unconscious may be dogmatic and superstitious, but this is a characteristic of the people involved, not of their concepts or way of speaking.

3 The concept of the unconscious is too simplistic

The idea that the division of the mind into conscious, preconscious and unconscious is too simplistic to capture the intricacies of mental life is probably true. The work of cognitive scientists like David Marr (1982), briefly described in Chapter 3, has demonstrated the existence of a whole array of unconscious mental processing systems that are certainly not done justice by Freud's basic tripartite division. However, the individuals who voice this objection do not strive to develop a more intricate, nuanced conception of the unconscious, but characteristically strive to replace Freud's three-fold division of the mind by something even more simplistic, claiming that the mind consists of nothing but *consciousness*. A tripartite division may well be crude, but a unipartite division is even cruder.

4 Freud's concept of the unconscious wasn't all that original

Although this is not, strictly speaking, a criticism of the unconscious, it seems appropriate to deal with it under this heading. Freud, it is said, was just one of many writers who discussed the unconscious, and his originality – and therefore the originality of the specifically psychoanalytic conception of the unconscious – has been grossly overstated. Remarks to this effect are generally accompanied by a reference to Henri Ellenberger's monumental *The Discovery of the*

Unconscious (1970). Although Ellenberger's book is in many ways excellent, and is probably indispensable to the serious student of the history of depth psychology, it also has severe limitations that are rarely mentioned. Ellenberger had a largely deflationist agenda, that is, he set out to redress what he rightly or wrongly took to be the excessive credit given to Freud at the expense of others who had written on the subject both prior to Freud and during his life-time. Ellenberger accomplished this by obliterating or minimizing distinctions. It is perfectly true that many writers, psychologists, philosophers and neuroscientists spoke about 'unconscious' or 'sub-conscious' mental states, but the *meanings* that they attached to these terms varied widely. When the philosopher Eduard von Hartmann, who is often mentioned in this context by people who have apparently never bothered to read him, speaks of the uncon-scious in abstract, metaphysical and quasi-religious terms this is a world apart from, say, the psychophysicist Gustav Fechner's account of the unconscious in terms of neurophysiological dispositions, and both stand in bold contrast to Freud's own formulations. The term 'unconscious' can cover a multitude of concepts and, as Wittgenstein felicitously put it, if one wraps various pieces of furniture in enough paper, they all end up looking the same. I have shown elsewhere (Smith, 1999a) that Freud's specific conception of the unconscious was radically different from those of most of his predecessors and contemporaries.

5 The unconscious is nothing but an imaginary place

The objection turns on the idea that the unconscious is a 'place' within the mind, but as the mind is non-spatial there can be no such thing as a mental location. Although grievously misconceived, this criticism might be suggested by Freud's 'topographical' model. After all, topography is a term for map-making, and maps represent places. This line of argument betrays both a very superficial reading of Freud and a deep ignorance about the nature and methodology of scientific model making. Scientific models are analogies for the phenomena that they are designed to represent. When a model makes use of spatial relationships, as do Freud's topography and countless other models in cognitive science, these spatial relation-ships metaphorically represent functional or causal relationships between mental processes or systems. Freud was actually quite explicit about this point, and was a long-standing opponent of the 'localizationist' doctrine that specific mental contents are located in specific areas of the mind-brain (Solms and Saling, 1986). In fact it is extremely difficult, and quite pointless, to talk about mental phenomena without making use of spatial metaphors. This is often done unreflectively, for instance when we speak of 'deep' or 'central' issues versus 'superficial' or 'peripheral' ones. To fault psychoanalysts for making use of a carefully articulated spatial model is thus an egregious example of mistaking the map for the territory.

6 Attributing actions to the unconscious is just a way of disclaiming responsibility for them

The idea here is that when we say that a piece of behaviour was caused by unconscious thoughts, intentions or fantasies it is much the same as saying 'the Devil made me do it'; that is, it is a method of disavowing ownership of and therefore responsibility for one's own actions and intentions and is at best a form of bad faith. As a criticism of the concept of the unconscious this objection is, to say the least, logically unsound. I am sure that there are people who use the unconscious as an excuse in this way, but this has no bearing whatsoever on the issue of the validity of the notion of the unconscious. After all, there are people who use real or confabulated illnesses as a way of evading responsibilities or obtaining special privileges, but this does not mean that there is no such thing as an illness. If I commit a crime and falsely blame it on my neighbour, it would be absurd for a third party to conclude that my neighbour therefore does not exist! And yet, this is precisely the logic used by those who question the existence of the unconscious simply because it is sometimes used as an excuse or rationalization.

7 Psychoanalytic arguments in support of the unconscious are circular

The claim here is that when psychoanalysts present evidence for the existence of the unconscious, they presuppose the existence of the very thing that they are attempting to demonstrate. Spinelli (1994), who attributes this argument to Wittgenstein and Sartre, expresses it as follows:

> In other words, they [psychoanalysts] argue if during psychoanalysis material is presented which it is claimed was once unconscious, the basis of this claim relies upon the hypothesis of an unconscious, for how else could the material be recognized as once-unconscious material. Clearly, even if we accept the notion of the unconscious, it remains the case that, at best, all that we ever directly confront is the 'unconscious made conscious'. But, if this is the case, then we cannot say that the existence has been proven. (150)

This excursion into philosophical criticism is multiply handicapped. In the first place, Spinelli uses a non-canonical approach to the validation of the notion of the unconscious. As we will see, Freudian arguments for the unconscious do *not* rest on the recovery of putatively unconscious memories. Freud argued that certain puzzling features of consciousness, such as dreams, 'slips', mental illness and creativity can best be explained by positing the existence of unconscious mental states and processes. Freud's reasoning was rather like that of Gregor Mendel, whose experiments selectively breeding pea plants suggested the existence of unobservable but nonetheless causally potent entities the existence of which was inferred on the basis of their effects. Mendel never directly observed a gene, just as Freud never observed an unconscious mental state, but both made inferences from the seen to the unseen. In light of this, Spinelli's argument misfires badly because he fails to engage with the relevant epistemological issues; but even if this were not the case, his argument would remain grievously flawed. If I were to recover a previously unknown but nevertheless genuine memory and go on to hold this out as evidence of the existence of unconscious mental states, I do not *presuppose* the existence of unconscious mental states, I *infer* that I had been unconscious of the memory prior to its emergence. Consider the following analogy. My wife comes into the house soaking wet and I conclude, without even looking out of the window, that it is raining outside. I do not *presuppose* that it is raining, but I infer it in much the same way that I infer that a previously unrecollected memory was unconscious prior to being recalled. Now, it could be said that I have to have the idea of rain already in my mind in order to make the inference that my wife's wetness is best explained by the hypothesis that it is raining, but this is true of *any* inference. I cannot infer something about which I have no prior conception. Spinelli's remarks about 'proving' the existence of the unconscious are a red herring. Science does not traffic in proof; it deals with more subtle, multifaceted and methodologically exacting issues of evidence.

8 Couldn't it just be ...?

All of the phenomena that psychoanalysts attribute to the action of unconscious mental states can be attributed to something else. Many and varied candidates have been put forward for this. Psychoanalysts, it is implied, must be remarkably hidebound to stick rigidly to their multiply-flawed notion of the unconscious in the face of so many intriguing options. As we have seen, it is a truism in the philosophy of science that theories are underdetermined by data. What this crisp statement means is that for any piece of data, there are a limitless number of explanations. Suppose that you were to take this book and drop it on the floor. Aristotle would understand the falling of the book as due to the book seeking out the centre of the earth, Isaac Newton would explain it as an effect of gravitational force, and Einstein would give an account based on the curvature of space. In fact, one could go on concocting explanations forever. The mere fact that there are alternative explanations for a phenomenon does not mean that these alternatives are good ones. It is incumbent upon the critic to demonstrate that the proffered explanation is at least as powerful as the theory that he or she seeks to displace. To his credit, Spinelli (1994) does seem to be aware of this requirement, but he does not carry it through in practice and does not seem to be aware of his failure to carry it through. Although Spinelli makes the ambitious claim that his alternative theory accommodates all of the clinical observations associated with psychoanalytic theories of the unconscious, he undertakes no survey of these clinical observations and remains mysteriously silent about Freud's *main* argument in favour of the unconscious (the 'continuity argument' described below). In light of his failure to deliver the goods, Spinelli's bold assertion can be regarded as little more than hand waving.

9. The theory of the unconscious is too reductionistic

The concept of reductionism is very poorly regarded in certain sectors of the contemporary intellectual scene. Like 'positivism', reductionism is said to be a Very Bad Thing and to be avoided at all costs. Any theory that embraces reductionism is, likewise, a bad theory that deserves to be renounced by all right-thinking people. Many, if not most, of the people who speak disparagingly about reductionism appear to be unaware of its philosophical pedigree and significance, much less the many volumes of thoughtful reflection that have been devoted to it.

Philosophers distinguish between various kinds of reductionism. The type of reductionism most relevant to this debate is called *ontological* reductionism. As we saw in Chapter 2, ontology is a philosophical term referring to what things *are*. Ontological reduction, then, is the attempt to explain things by analysing them into their constituent parts. The classic example of ontological reduction is the explanation of temperature as the mean kinetic energy. Here the macro-property (temperature) is explained by a property of its constituent micro-entities (molecules). It should be apparent that virtually all scientific explanation is in some sense reductionistic. Reductionism has accordingly been described as the most successful research strategy ever devised (Medawar, 1982).

Those who accuse psychoanalysis of being 'too reductionistic' do not normally have a principled objection to reductionism *per se*. They do not object to reductionism in physics, and are happy to enjoy the fruits of technological progress that are based on scientific reductionism. These critics simply object to the use of reductionistic strategies to explain the human mind. But they do not appear to have any real justification as to just why reductionism is to be avoided in this, and only this, domain. I think there may be a not-so-covert agenda here. If reductionism is taboo, then the scientific understanding of the mind is also out of bounds. However, if we are denied a scientific understanding of the mind we encounter the problems raised in our previous discussion of hermeneutics, namely that we then have no means of acquiring objective and reliable knowledge of the mind. The objection to the theory of the unconscious on the grounds of its reductionism is an expression of a retrograde and reactionary philosophical agenda. Those who oppose 'reductionistic psychology' apparently wish to retain the illusion that human beings inhabit a privileged position in the cosmic scheme. They greet psychoanalysis with the same resistance with which their forebears once greeted Copernicus, who displaced us from the centre of the universe, and Darwin, who showed us that we are animals.

Serious objections and refutations

Because most nineteenth century thinkers believed that all mental states are conscious, they argued that what seemed to be unconscious mental activity was either not really unconscious or not really mental. The first option, called 'dissociationism', involved claiming that consciousness itself can become split or dissociated, and that each split-off piece of consciousness is fully conscious of itself, but does not have access to what is going on inside the others. A single skull is supposedly able to house several selves, consciousnesses or personalities. The most famous advocate of this theory, although he later repudiated it, was Pierre Janet. The American psychologist William James translated Janet's '*desegregation*' into 'dissociation' and introduced it into the English-language literature, where it has recently been revived in the wake of resurgent interest in so-called dissociative disorders.

The second option was to admit that the states in question are really unconscious, but to deny that they are mental. According to this 'dispositionalist' view, so-called unconscious mental states are not really mental at all: they are purely physical states of the nervous system and should be spoken of in purely neurophysiological terms; what we misleadingly call an 'unconscious fantasy' is, in reality, a set of neural processes which, were they allowed to develop fully, might give rise to a conscious and therefore truly mental state.

In contrast to these two options, which have their advocates even today, Freud asserted that truly mental states can be radically, intrinsically unconscious. Given that any purported example of an unconscious mental state can in principle be interpreted as an example of split consciousness or of a neurophysiological disposition, Freud's justifications for the concept of the unconscious are for the most part philosophical ones aimed at showing that his conception provided a more powerful and elegant explanation of the phenomena in question than its rivals.

Many of Freud's contemporaries rejected the idea of unconscious mental events on the grounds that something mental cannot, as a matter of definition, be unconscious. To put it another way, they held that 'conscious' is part of the meaning of the term 'mental', and to speak of unconscious mental contents is therefore to contradict oneself. Freud dismissed this as a 'trifling matter of definition' (1905b). He strongly objected to the idea that psychology must be constrained by the conventions of ordinary language (Freud, 1905b; 1912a; 1913; 1916–17; 1923a; 1925; 1940a). Science seeks to expand our understanding of the universe. It cannot do this without also expanding the way that we talk about the universe. Again, there are many examples of this in physics. The idea that time itself was created in the Big Bang and that 'before' the Big Bang time did not exist sounds, to laypersons' ears, like a contradiction in terms, and yet this very notion is fundamental to modern cosmology. Again, the neuroscientific idea that thoughts are electro-chemical events within the brain contradicts the widespread notion that thoughts do not have physical properties. The semantic argument could be taken more seriously if it were literally impossible to imagine an unconscious mental state, in the same way that it is impossible to imagine a four-sided triangle. But this is clearly not the case. To say that 'a triangle has three sides' is a tautology, the most fundamental form of logical truth, but to say that 'a mental state is conscious' is not.

Freud mounted arguments against both the dissociationist and dispositionalist theories. He attacked dispositionalism using a strategy that I have named the 'Continuity Argument' (Smith, 1999b), which is based on the observation that the stream of consciousness is riddled with 'gaps'. Not only do we go to sleep each night, and wake up with our thoughts, memories and personal identities intact, even during periods when we are fully conscious, our minds sometimes jump back and forth from one subject to another. A particularly dramatic and suggestive example of mental discontinuity is the experience of 'sleeping on' a problem and waking up with an answer. During the period of sleep one was not working consciously on the problem, but the unbidden appearance of a solution suggests that unconscious work was being done on it during the night. Sometimes, we put a problem out of mind without sleeping on it, and an answer suddenly and unexpectedly emerges into consciousness, sometimes days later.

The literature on scientific creativity (Hadamard, 1949) is rich in examples of this kind. A famous example was recorded by the great French physicist Henri Poincaré, who abandoned work on a seemingly intractable mathematical problem to take a holiday break. Poincaré recounts that:

> Having reached Coustances, we entered an omnibus to go some place or other. At the moment I put my foot on the step the idea came to me, without anything in my former thoughts seeming to have paved the way for it, that the transformations I had used to define the Fuchsian functions were identical to those of non-Euclidian geometry. I did not verify the idea; I should not have had time, as, upon taking my seat in the omnibus, I went on with a conversation already commenced, but I felt a perfect certainty. On my return to Caen, for conscience's sake I verified the result at my leisure. (1913: 383–4)

It seems obvious that Poincaré had been working on the problem unconsciously. How else could he have arrived at the solution? There was a substantial temporal gap between the moment that he gave up working on the problem and the moment when the answer popped into his head, and there was clearly a causal link between his mental states at these two moments, otherwise we would have to assume that Poincaré's solution came upon him completely by chance, which is absurd. Now, given the fact that Poincaré did not know the solution when he gave up on the problem to go to Coustances, it is reasonable to conclude that he must have thought more about the problem between this time and his moment of enlightenment on the omnibus and, as he was not conscious of doing this, his thought processes must have been *unconscious*.

How would the dispositionalist explain this example? He would have to build the case that only non-mental neurophysiological processes occurred during the period between the two events, and that there was no thinking involved in this sequence at all. But if this were the case, how did Poincaré reach his solution? As the saying goes, 'if it walks like a duck and quacks like a duck, it's a duck': whatever went on unconsciously during the interval looks a lot like a mental process, and it seems that only the prejudice that mental processes must be conscious stands in the way of accepting this.

Freud did not mount such a sustained attack on dissociationism, but he nonetheless made some telling points. Freud questioned the coherence of the notion of 'a consciousness of which its own possessor knows nothing' (1915c: 170): an 'unconscious consciousness'. The nineteenth century literature expressed this as the distinction between a person's primary or main consciousness, and their secondary (or tertiary, quaternary ...) consciousness.

Returning to the Poincaré example, the dissociationist would have to assert that Poincaré seemed to be unconscious of his mathematical reflections because it was his secondary consciousness that did the work. Poincaré's primary consciousness was unaware of the existence of his secondary consciousness, which gave the impression that the work was carried out unconsciously. Somehow his secondary consciousness managed to convey the solution to his primary consciousness aboard the omnibus in Coustances.

Freud raised several objections against this kind of explanation. First, he questioned the very idea that the hypothesis of an unconscious consciousness can be evidentially supported. Even if the mind can be divided into two or more sub-minds, there seems to be no way to establish whether these are actually centres of consciousness. Simply insisting that they are conscious seems to be based on the dogmatic 'preconceived belief that regards the identity of the psychical and the conscious as settled once and for all' (Freud, 1923a: 16n) rather than on evidence. The idea of unconscious consciousnesses also violates the time-honoured principle of Occam's Razor. As Freud astutely observed, postulating the existence of more than one consciousness residing within a single cranium gives us licence to 'assume the existence not only of a second consciousness, but of a third, fourth, perhaps of an unlimited number of states of consciousness, all unknown to us and to one another' (Freud, 1915c: 170). This insight was elegantly developed, quite independently of Freud, by the British philosopher Peter Strawson (Strawson, 1974). Strawson stressed that consciousness does not *inhabit* people but is a *property* of them, just as the redness of a rose is not an entity contained *in* the rose, but is a property *of* the rose, pointing out that if there were 'consciousnesses' lurking inside of us there would be no way, even in principle, of counting them. It would be impossible even to track whether the consciousness inhabiting someone at one moment is the same one inhabiting them at the next moment. In fact, there would be no obstacle to postulating that there are a million consciousnesses, all with identical experiences, inhabiting a person all at once or a single consciousness inhabiting a million people all at once. Such a brief account cannot really do justice to the elegance of Strawson's analysis, and the interested reader can consult the original. Suffice it to say that Strawson confirms Freud's claim that the floodgates are opened as soon as one postulates multiple consciousnesses. Furthermore, Freud emphasizes that we 'play havoc' with 'the one and only piece of direct and certain knowledge that we have about the mind' when we speak of consciousness as something that can be unconscious (Freud, 1923a: 16n). The direct and certain knowledge to which Freud refers, echoing Descartes' *Meditations*, is the experience of consciousness.

Freud's last (1915c) objection to the dissociationist hypothesis was based on a purported dissimilarity between conscious and unconscious mental processes. Freud believed that many unconscious processes possess characteristics that are radically different to those that we associate with the conscious domain. In other words, unconscious cognition is not simply conscious cognition minus the element of consciousness. If the nature of conscious mentation is so very different from the nature of what we take to be unconscious mental processes, if the former possesses cognitive properties not possessed by the latter, this should make us cautious about assuming that phenomenologically unconscious mental states possess a consciousness of their own. Although Freud felt that this final consideration is the most powerful of the three, this is not really true. His first two objections are theory-neutral: in fact, one can agree with them without any commitment to specifically psychoanalytic theories of the mind, whereas the third objection requires prior acceptance of the validity of Freudian ideas about unconscious mental processes.

As we have already noted, another alternative to the idea of unconscious mental events is the notion that these are best explained by *gradations* of consciousness. According to this view, consciousness can be more or less intense; as though there were a dimmer switch controlling it, and that so-called unconscious ideas are just items that we are only slightly or marginally conscious of. Perhaps Poincaré was only peripherally conscious of his ongoing thoughts about the problem. This may be theoretically possible, but if it was the case in this example, then Poincaré was unaware of it. Of course, if Poincaré were unaware that he was marginally aware of what he was thinking, then we are back to the dissociationist conception of an unconscious consciousness against which objections have already been raised. Freud's own refutation was that the mere fact that there are gradations in consciousness, although plausible, has no bearing whatsoever on the question of the existence of unconscious mental states, remarking that this 'has no more evidential value than such analogous statements as "There are so very many gradations in illumination … therefore there is no such thing as darkness at all"' (1923a: 16n).

Irrationality and the attribution problem

One of the distinctive characteristics of the psychoanalytic conception of the unconscious is the idea of its radical irrationality. The idea of an irrational unconscious is widely appealing, and for good reason. Human beings appear often to behave irrationally. If the very core of the human mind were irrational, this would at least appear to explain a good deal about human nature. Or would it?

Freud conceived of the unconscious in at least two distinct ways. At times, he described unconscious thinking as rational and capable of intellectual problem solving, in the way illustrated by the Poincaré example given above. Most of Freud's works describe System Unconscious, and later on the id, as radically irrational and dominated by the blind quest for satisfaction. It is this distinctively psychoanalytic conception of the 'dynamic' unconscious that raises fundamental problems for psychoanalysis.

The psychoanalytic unconscious is said to lie between the drives on one hand and consciousness and behaviour on the other. The drives themselves are not unconscious in the Freudian sense of the word because they are physiological rather than mental states. These physiological forces impelling us to seek sexual as well as aggressive satisfaction are mediated by the unconscious. As Ernest Gellner evocatively describes it, 'The Unconscious … is a kind of gearbox, in which the tremendous force of the elemental drives within us can mesh into the complex, intricate and fragile meanings in terms of which we live' (Gellner, 1985: 109). Having gained access to the unconscious, many of these 'dark bio-forces' (ibid.) are prevented from direct expression, and are transformed and neutralized by processes such as displacement, condensation and symbolization as well as a whole host of defence mechanisms to create dreams, character traits, 'slips' and so on. Freud was quite explicit that this biologically driven unconscious is essentially irrational. As he succinctly put it in *The Ego and the Id* (1923a: 73), 'The logical laws of thought do not apply in the id.' If some psychoanalytic interpretations appear to be far-fetched by the standards of conscious thought, this is because in the unconscious anything can stand for anything else. This is why the id is described as 'a chaos, a seething cauldron full of excitations' (ibid.) devoid of any internal organization.

Normally when we attribute mental states to others we do so with the help of a basic framework of rationality. We have to *assume* basic rationality if we are to make any sense at all of anyone's actions. Rationality, in this sense, means a logical coherence between most of a person's desires and beliefs. So, as in the example of Winston mentioned above, if we see someone pour themself a cool drink and avidly guzzle it down we infer that (a) they were thirsty, and (b) that they believed that consuming a cool drink would slake their thirst. It is the tight, logical relationship between actions, beliefs and desires that provides the framework of rationality by means of which we interpret others. Now, here is the problem. According to psychoanalytic theory the unconscious (or the id) does not operate within a framework of rationality: it is fundamentally non-rational, unstructured and non-logical. But if there are no normative structures constraining the relationship between unconscious mental states and behaviour, in short, if the way that the unconscious is expressed is entirely 'up for grabs', then it is difficult to understand how it is possible to make secure inferences about unconscious mental states. It would appear that if the psychoanalytic unconscious exists, and possesses the irrational properties that Freud and others have attributed to it, that unconscious is for the most part *unknowable* and there is no real rational basis for the psychoanalytic interpretations of dreams, symptoms, free associations and so on. This problem has rarely been voiced in the psychoanalytic literature (Smith, 1999a) and has, to the best of my knowledge, never been answered.

The psychoanalytic unconscious and the cognitive unconscious

There are significant overlaps between aspects of psychoanalytic and cognitivist thinking about the mind. As we have seen, many contemporary cognitivists routinely invoke unconscious mental processes for explanatory purposes. There are also specific theoretical concepts upon which psychoanalytic and cognitivist ideas meet in rather startling ways. To give but one example, Freud's writings on consciousness, although relatively unknown territory for most psychoanalysts, dovetail with much recent work in cognitive neuroscience and cognitive linguistics (Smith, 2000). Given their common emphasis on mental processes occurring outside of awareness, it may be tempting for the psychoanalytic apologist to pronounce that psychoanalysis has been at least partially validated by cognitive science. This conclusion would not be warranted. Problems arise as soon as we get down to specifics about just what kinds of items are unconscious in psychoanalytic and cognitivist theories of the mind. On the whole, psychoanalysts talk about unconscious sexual conflicts, dreads, shameful memories, wishes and fantasies – in short, mental *contents* – whereas cognitive scientists are characteristically concerned with unconscious algorithms, information-processing routines and rules such as the steps in Marr's theory of visual processing described in Chapter 3. The cognitive unconscious is, as it were, cool and dry, whereas the psychoanalytic unconscious is hot and wet. Cognitive scientists talk about unconscious processes and contents that are emotionally neutral and incapable of, even in principle, becoming conscious, whereas the psychoanalytic unconscious is chock-full of emotionally excruciating thoughts that can, at least in principle if not in practice, be admitted into consciousness. So, although both the psychoanalytic and cognitivist domains of enquiry include the unconscious, the similarity may end here (Eagle, 1987). This conclusion may be unduly pessimistic. Although at present the gap between cognitivist and psychoanalytic conceptions is a large one, this may be partially due to the fact that it is only very recently that cognitive science has begun consistently to investigate affectively significant mental phenomena. There are certainly aspects of psychoanalytic theory which bear on traditional cognitive scientific concerns such as the neural instantiation of thoughts, the relationship between thought and consciousness, the neural basis of conscious experience and so on (Smith, 1999a, 2000), just as there are cognitive scientists who investigate emotionally significant mental events and unconscious communication (Haskell, 1999, 2001). The jury is still out on the degree to which these investigations will confirm or contradict psychoanalytic propositions.

Accessing the unconscious

Although the conception of the unconscious has, on the whole, fared rather well against the slings and arrows of its critics, the related issue of how psychoanalysts gain knowledge of the unconscious has shown itself to be far more vulnerable.

Freud described dreams as a royal road to the knowledge of the unconscious activities of the mind. If dreams are the royal road, then the free association method is the vehicle that drives down it. Dreams, slips, neurotic symptoms and creativity can all provide this knowledge only if they are examined using the appropriate tools. In psychoanalysis, the tool used is the method of free association. Freud described free association as the 'fundamental rule' of psychoanalysis, an epithet that aptly describes its crucial role in psychoanalytic technique. It is, in the words of Adolf Grünbaum (1997: 338), 'the supposed microscope and X-ray tomograph of the human mind'. As such, the integrity of the free association method supports a good portion of the epistemic weight of the psychoanalytic skyscraper. If the method is proven to be questionable, or at least precarious, then a considerable amount of psychoanalytic theory will thereby be shown to have been built upon sand. Given its foundational status, one would expect to find a large psychoanalytic literature discussing the method and its uses. In fact, methodological discussions of free association are few, cursory and far between because the value and proper deployment of the method are taken largely for granted by proponents of psychoanalysis, with little or no effort at justification. This blithe methodological self-assurance is not really justified. As we will see, there are several very telling critiques of the psychoanalytic uses of free association that have never been adequately countered, or apparently even considered, by the vast majority of psychoanalytic theorists and practitioners.

Let us first be clear about exactly what free association consists of. The term is an English rendering of Freud usually called 'freier Einfall' in the German. 'Freier', of course, means 'free' but 'Einfall' does not have a precise English equivalent. It is best understood as the involuntary intrusion of thoughts into consciousness, as when a thought pops into one's mind 'out of the blue'. 'Freier Einfall', then, is the process of allowing thoughts to freely come to mind. Freud (1904) described it as follows:

> Without exerting any other kind of influence, he [Freud] ... asks the patient to 'let himself go' in what he says, 'as you would do in a conversation in which you were rambling on quite disconnectedly and at random'. Before he asks them for a detailed account of their case history, he insists that they must include in it whatever comes into their heads, even if they think it unimportant or irrelevant or nonsensical; he lays special stress on their not omitting any thought or idea from their story because to relate it would be embarrassing or distressing

to them. In the course of collecting this material of otherwise
neglected ideas, Freud made the observations that became the determining factor of his entire theory. (250–51)

The free association method is based on the principle of psychical
determinism, which was introduced in the preceding chapter. Freud's
adherence to psychical determinism was deeply rooted in his philosophical materialism. He held that the mind is ultimately identical
with the brain and is therefore a purely physical system, and as such
its operations are not random but are governed by the causal laws
that determine the behaviour of all other material objects in the
universe (with the possible exception of subatomic particles). It follows
that those ideas that seem to randomly pop into one's head for no
reason are actually the effects of deeper, unconscious causes. They
are, according to psychoanalytic reasoning, disguised or encoded
expressions of repressed thoughts. Freud believed that unconscious
ideas are indirectly expressed through conscious substitutes that he
called 'derivatives'. The purpose of free association is to give the
analyst maximum access to derivatives, so as to provide ample raw
material for making inferences about deeper unconscious issues. As
Freud put it in *The Interpretation of Dreams* (1900), 'when conscious purposive ideas are abandoned, concealed purposive ideas
assume control of the current of ideas' (1900: 531). Free association
is the analytic patient's main role responsibility and the analyst's
main investigative instrument. If it turns out to be seriously flawed,
this would cast doubt on psychoanalysis as a theory, as a therapy
and as a method of research.

Adolf Grünbaum has shown us how Freud used the purported
therapeutic effects of psychoanalysis to give his theories scientific
credibility. The same principle also applies to his justification of
psychoanalytic methods, notably the method of free association.
Psychoanalysts endorse the free association method because they
believe that patients' associations allow them to access pathogenic
repressed ideas and subsequently bring these into consciousness.
Two crucial inferences flowing from this proposition are (1) if psychoanalytic cure is brought about by means of lifting repression, it follows
that emotional disorders are *caused* by pathogenic repression in the
first place, and (2) if this is the case, and if the free association
method is uniquely capable of uncovering repression, then the free
association method is a unique tool for identifying the causes of
emotional disorders.

Freud's argument breaks down for the following reasons. First,
even if it is true that the lifting of repression brings about the cessation

of neurotic symptoms it does not follow that repression was the cause of the symptoms. Analogously, just because taking aspirin removes a headache this does not mean that the headache was caused by an aspirin deficiency. Second, this claim does not cohere with the therapeutic track record of psychoanalysis. As we have seen, even Freud (1937) admitted a few years before his death that it is quite rare for psychoanalysis to produce complete, lasting cures, and that the therapeutic effects of psychoanalysis are actually quite modest. Of course, it might be objected that great progress has been made since Freud's time and that the therapeutic acuity of psycho-analysis has been honed by subsequent generations of analysts. Freud was himself critical of this 'optimistic' view (1937) and his pes-simism is entirely justified by present-day outcome research, which provides no empirical evidence vindicating the claim that psycho-analysis possesses uniquely potent therapeutic powers. Third, when therapeutic improvement, however great or small, does take place during psychoanalytic treatment, it is not clear that this improve-ment has occurred as a result of the dissolution of repression. Again, as we have seen above, therapeutic improvements might be more accurately attributed to the effects of suggestion, as well as a host of other factors. Therapeutic improvement taking place during or as a result of psychoanalytic therapy cannot reasonably be laid at the door of the free association method unless plausible competing explanations have been effectively ruled out.

Leaving aside the problematic issue of therapeutic effects, what other grounds are there for endorsing the power of free association to unearth unconscious mental contents? According to psycho-analytic theory, when one freely associates on a dream image, a slip of the tongue and so on, one's associations will, unless obstructed by resistances, move inexorably towards the very issues which were the cause of the dream (or slip, symptom and so forth) and are consti-tutive of its latent meaning. For example, I once dreamed that I was Ronald Reagan sitting behind a large desk. Free-associating to the dream, I recalled that the desk in the dream closely resembled a desk that my father purchased for me when I was doing poorly in secondary school and in danger of failing. This realization led to thoughts about having recently applied for a job and my fear that I would not be accepted for it. A psychoanalyst might conclude that this dream was brought about by suppressed fears of failing in my effort to get the job, which were influenced by and evocative of the memories of humiliating failure earlier in my life (for a more detailed analysis of this dream see Smith, 1999b). There can be no doubt that the free association process led me to rich, emotionally significant material, but does this validate psychoanalytic claims about the powers of free association? No, it doesn't. To understand why not, consider the following observation by Ludwig Wittgenstein:

> The fact is that whenever you are preoccupied with something, with some trouble or with some problem which is a big thing in your life – as sex is, for instance – then no matter what you start from, the association will lead finally and inevitably back to that same theme. (1966: 50–51)

So, even if we grant that free association regularly leads to thoughts about emotionally significant concerns and conflicts, this is not sufficient evidence to establish that these concerns caused or in any way underpinned the dream, slip, symptom or whatever phenomenon the chain of associations began from. The assumption that free association reveals the underlying cause and meaning of a mental phenomenon falls foul of the logical fallacy of *post hoc ergo propter hoc*. The mere fact that one event is preceded by another does not license the inference that the former caused the latter. Rosemary Sand, a retired psychoanalyst and critic of her profession, sums up the problem concisely as follows:

> Why should a series of associations to pieces of a dream give you the 'background thoughts' of those pieces? How can you assume that a series of thoughts which *follow* a dream will lead you to the thoughts which *preceded* the dream? No doubt, a series of thoughts will lead you *somewhere*, but you cannot justifiably assume that you have been led to the background thoughts which produced the dream. (1993: 530)

Sand argues that the conventional psychoanalytic belief that free association throws light upon and epistemologically certifies inferences about the causes and meanings of dreams is justified neither by logic nor by evidence: its truth is simply *assumed* by proponents of psychoanalytic practice. She calls this the 'free association fallacy', while others use the more general epithet 'fallacy of causal reversal' (Glymour, 1983; Grünbaum, 1984). From this perspective, the unfolding of a meaningful train of associations from, say, a dream image no more certifies the unconscious causes and meaning of the image than the fact that I brush my teeth before going to bed establishes that brushing my teeth causes me to go to bed.

Here one might object that the non-psychological example of going to bed and brushing my teeth is not an appropriate one. Consider a second example that may be more pertinent, that of Winston recognizing that he is thirsty and then going to the refrigerator to get a glass of ginger beer. In this case, any sane person will concur that the thought 'I am thirsty and want some ginger beer' caused Winston to get up off the sofa, open the refrigerator and pour himself a glass of ginger beer, and that if he had not been aware of his thirst he would never have got up to get a drink. What seems to justify this inference is the *thematic affinity* between the thought of drinking ginger beer and the act of drinking ginger beer. His thought of drinking ginger beer is directly mirrored in his action.

The ginger beer example is a very strong one. In psychoanalytic practice the thematic resonances are at best somewhat more tenuous and obscure. However, even in very strong cases the argument from thematic affinity proves to be misleading. Grünbaum (1993) argues that even in examples like Winston and the ginger beer, the issue of thematic affinity is a red herring for the following reason. Consider the example of Elaine waking up one morning and thinking 'I am going to win the Lottery' and then going on to purchase a ticket bearing the numbers revealed to her in a dream. These turn out to be the winning numbers, and Elaine wins the jackpot. In this example there is a very strong thematic affinity between the thought about winning the lottery and the event of actually winning it, but it would not be reasonable to conclude that the thought *caused* Elaine to win the lottery. Why not? Because we know that it is a far more frequent occurrence for people to think that they are going to win the lottery and then go on to lose it. In the example featuring Winston, however, we know from *prior experience* that when people think that they want a drink they are inclined, all things being equal, to get themselves a drink. According to Grünbaum, all such warranted causal attributions turn out in the final analysis to rest on prior empirical observations. We draw the conclusions that we do because of our previous experiences. If this seems far-fetched, it is only because we take such prior knowledge so completely for granted in our everyday lives. Grünbaum (1993) hammers this point home with what has become a classic example: someone walking on a deserted beach and noticing what appear to be two human footprints in the sand. He concludes that another person has been on the beach, but what is his basis for doing so?

> The striking geometric kinship between the two shapes does not itself suffice to license the tourist's inference that the foot*like* configurations were, in fact, caused … by the impact of human feet on the beach. To draw that inference the tourist avails himself of a crucial piece of *additional* information: Footlike beach formations in the sand

never or hardly ever result from the 'mere chance' collocation of sand particles under the action of the air, such as some gust of wind. (130)

As we have seen in Chapter 2, psychoanalysts simply do not have the prior empirical knowledge that would enable them to make causal inferences about phenomena such as dreams, neurotic symptoms and so on. The argument from thematic affinity is doomed to failure.

There is another principle invoked by psychoanalysts to support and supplement the use of free association. They sometimes argue that the skilled interpretation of free associations yields a uniquely complex and coherent account of the patient's inner life, and it is this fact that makes inferences guided by thematic affinities more secure. It is not just the thematic affinity that carries the epistemic burden of an interpretation, it is this conjoined with the capacity of an interpretation to paint a much more comprehensive and intelligible picture of the patient's psychological universe than would otherwise be possible. We have already encountered this 'jigsaw puzzle' argument and found it wanting. Conjoining one inadequate justification with another does not add up to anything more than the sum of the two parts. The same general objection was raised by Wittgenstein (1966) with respect to the psychoanalytic method for interpreting dreams.

> Freud remarks how, after the analysis of it, the dream appears so very logical. And of course it does. You could start with any of the objects on this table – which are certainly not put there through your dream activity – and you could find that they all could be connected in a pattern like that; and the pattern would be logical in the same way. (51)

A stronger elucidation of the same point was made by the philosopher Clarke Glymour (1993) in a scathing analysis of Freud's approach to the interpretation of dreams.

> If a person is asked to associate his thoughts with elements of a dream, and report his associations, after a while we will be able to make up a cogent story, thought, fear, wish or whatever from the resulting associations. We know that simply from our elementary psychological knowledge of people. There is nothing special about dreams in this regard; much the same could be done with rock formations, or with blotches of ink. ... Now the production of such associations from dream elements and the resulting stories will do nothing to establish that the *dreams* are expressing that story, that thought, any more than the stories that result from people observing random ink blots or rock formations and then associating freely give evidence that the ink blots or the rock formations are expressing those stories. (60–61)

Paranoid persons have a highly developed aptitude for fabricating stories linking together what are in fact disparate and unconnected phenomena into impressively coherent narratives, generating conspiracy theories and the like. Although paranoid narratives have the remarkable property of extracting at least the appearance of order out of chaos they remain, in the final analysis, delusions. The art of making 'connections' is like the art of seeing the shapes in the clouds: they are testimony to nothing more than the creative imagination of the viewer. Free association provides such a rich stream of thoughts, memories and fantasies that it would be very surprising if a seasoned practitioner trained in the art of weaving together psychoanalytic narratives were unable to make a meaningful story out of them.

Even if we were to grant, for the sake of the argument, that psychoanalytic interpretations are not merely imaginative creations by the analyst but actually reflect the covert or implicit content of an analysand's free associations, we are still confronted with the problematic issue of epistemic contamination. To what extent are analysands' 'free' associations moulded by subtle (or not so subtle) cues communicated by the analyst? Grünbaum has shown that Freud was unable to eliminate the possibility that psychoanalytic cures can be put down to the operation of suggestion, and neither he nor analysts coming after him have been able to counter the charge that the very material produced by analysands may be in large measure sculpted by the analyst's expectations. But if this were the case, then it would hardly be surprising to discover that these very free associations conform rather well to analysts' theoretical beliefs!

As long ago as 1943, the veteran psychoanalyst Wilhelm Stekel remarked that 'If the patient is continually being badgered concerning infantile traumata, he will dream about them abundantly' (Stekel, 1943: 314). Stekel's example of confirmatory dreams is poorly chosen as a criticism of Freudian analysis for the simple reason that Freud's theory of dreaming specifically *predicts* it. According to Freud, the *manifest* content of dreams is largely made up of impressions from the day preceding the dream, which he termed 'day-residues'. Anyone in intensive psychotherapy is likely to have day-residues from his or her psychotherapy sessions, which are then taken up into their dreams. Strictly speaking, it is actually antithetical to Freudian theory to treat the manifest content of a dream as confirmatory, given that psychoanalysts regard the manifest content as merely a disguise for the hidden, latent content of the dream. Be that as it may, psychoanalysts do not realize the degree to which their patients' 'free' associations may be under the sway of their own unwitting suggestive influence, and therefore the extent to which the content of these very associations, 'insights' and other ostensibly confirmatory clinical phenomena may in fact be little more than arte-facts of the clinical situation. The psychoanalyst Judd Marmor (1962) has remarked, in the passage quoted on page 32, that patients tend to produce precisely the kind of data described by their analysts' theories.

Although we should not take this proposition on board just because Marmor says it, his remarks are at least *credible*, particu-larly when considered in light of the experimental literature demon-strating just how suggestible normal human beings can be if they are subjected to the right kind of pressure. Solomon Asch (1956) carried out a classic series of experiments in which subjects were shown several pairs of lines. The members of one of the pairs were obvi-ously the same length, whereas another equally obviously consisted of lines of different lengths. The experimenter was, unbeknownst to the subject, assisted by nine co-conspirators who were instructed to claim that the matching lines were of different lengths and the mismatched lines were of the same length. Asch found that a full 75 per cent of his subjects concurred with an obviously false major-ity opinion. But there was something deeper going on here than the need to outwardly conform to peer pressure. Many of Asch's subjects told him that they had actually *seen* the mismatched lines as equal and the equal lines as mismatched! In other similarly constructed experiments, subjects were induced to see the colour blue as green (Bloom, 2000). Suggestibility cuts deep, influencing not only what we say, but also what we perceive.

It can be argued that as impressive as these results are as a demonstration of the malleability of the human mind, they are stud-ies of group processes and therefore in important respects unrepre-sentative of the one-to-one psychoanalytic setting. Against this, it can be said that the psychoanalytic situation is not necessarily less psychically coercive than Asch's experimental set-up and is, given its admittedly transference-laden character, arguably more so. Fortunately, we need not speculate on these matters, as there exists good experimental research tracking the influence of suggestion in settings more closely akin to the one-to-one psychoanalytic encounter. Elizabeth Loftus, the psychologist and expert on memory who has done so much to debunk the 'recovered memory' industry, conducted an experiment in which she showed college students a film of a traffic accident and then asked them 'How fast was the white car going when it passed the barn?' The students were later asked about what happened in the film, and 17 per cent mentioned the car passing a barn, whereas in fact there were no buildings of any kind in the film.

> In a related experiment students were shown a collision between a bicycle and an auto driven by a brunette, then afterwards were peppered with questions about the 'blonde' at the steering wheel. Not only did they remember the nonexistent blonde vividly, but when they were shown the video a second time, they had a hard time believing that it was the same incident they now recalled so graphically. One subject said, 'It's really strange because I still have the blonde girl's face in my mind and it doesn't correspond to her [pointing to the woman on the video screen]. ... It was really weird.' (Bloom, 2000: 73)

Given Freud's point that the positive transference, which is a *sine qua non* of psychoanalytic treatment, greatly increases patients' suggestibility, it is not at all far-fetched to assume that patients' free associations are likely to be subtly influenced by their analysts' expectations.

Freud's main defence of the free association method is a version of the argument from the consilience of inductions that might be called the argument from converging associations. He believed that when two or more chains of association having their points of departure in separate elements of a dream unexpectedly converge on a single idea, this associative crossroads supplies a valuable key to the latent meaning of the dream. Consider Freud's interpretation of a dream presented by one of his patients in which she was preparing to give a dinner-party but had no food in the house except a little smoked salmon. The dreamer told Freud that she had recently visited a female friend of whom her husband was disconcertingly fond. The dreamer's husband was attracted to plump women, but her friend was reassuringly thin. The dreamer then recalled an occasion when the thin friend had spoken about wanting to gain weight, and asked the patient when she was going to invite her over for a meal. After hearing these associations, Freud interpreted the dream as expressing the patient's wish that her friend remain slim. The dreamer responded that smoked salmon was her favourite food! With this final association both the element of the dinner-party and the image of smoked salmon unexpectedly converge on the patient's friend. It is as if two witnesses have independently identified a criminal, thereby enhancing the credence of both testimonies. Unfortunately, as Glymour (1983) demonstrates, this impression may be more apparent than real. Although it may *seem* that the woman's emotionally charged thoughts about her skinny friend obviously generated the images of the dinner party and the smoked salmon, what may be really going on is that the dreamer freely associated until she hit on something that happened to be associated with several elements of her dream. It was not the thought of her friend that caused her to dream of the inadequate dinner party and the smoked salmon. Instead, it was the thought of the dinner-party and the smoked salmon that led the dreamer to think about her friend. Looked at in this way, psychoanalysts may be guilty of committing the fallacy of causal inversion every time that they use the convergence of associations to interpret the latent meaning of a dream. Freud used the patient's associations to search for a common denominator for the two dream elements, but this does not suffice to establish a causal linkage between them. The jazz musician Charley Parker was nicknamed 'Bird', and Charles Darwin studied Galapagos finches. There is a link between them through their Christian names and their connection with birds. Does this attest to some deep relationship between them? No, it only goes to show that a careful search can reveal all sorts of associative linkages between unrelated thoughts.

The criticisms offered by Wittgenstein, Sand, Grünbaum, Glymour and others do not entail that psychoanalytic interpretations of free associations are false; they merely assert that Freudian reasoning is not adequate to support the claim that they are true. It is also important to bear in mind that the arguments do not claim that the practice of free association is psychotherapeutically unproductive, or that it does not help patients gain deeper insights into their emotional life. Any method that helps one to reflect on emotional conflicts is *a priori* psychologically enriching, but this is a far cry from establishing the causal credentials of the conflicts so discovered.

Even if all of the preceding objections to the free association were shown to be ill considered, there would still be very strong grounds for rejecting psychoanalytic interpretations based on the use of the free association method, because even if we grant that free associations throw light on the unconscious sources of dreams, slips, symptoms and the like, the awkward fact remains that there is no explicit and consistent methodology for interpreting the associations. The process of interpretation remains such an idiosyncratic procedure that it is doubtful whether a panel of psychoanalysts exposed to an identical set of free associations would unanimously come up with the same, or even similar, interpretations of them. As Glymour notes, there are no rules for how to piece associations together into stories, no rules for stopping the dreamer's associations, for urging him to continue

or for coming back to a dream image and soliciting further associations. Given this laxness, the psychoanalyst is in the position of
being able to stop the associations at will or, conversely, insist that
they continue, so as to obtain associations that fit any preferred
interpretation.

The only strictly *clinical* concept that is arguably as close to the
heart of psychoanalysis as is the concept of the unconscious is the
notion of transference, and its counterpart countertransference. I
will argue in Chapter 6 that although they are rarely questioned, the
concepts of transference and countertransference may well provide
only very insecure foundations for clinical practice.

6
Transference and Countertransference in Focus

Transference is widely regarded as being at the core of psychoanalytic technique: Freud's 'grandest clinical hypothesis' (Luborsky et al., 1985). It is also one of the rare psychoanalytic concepts that is endorsed even by some of the discipline's most vitriolic critics. 'There is,' remarks by Ernest Gellner (1985), the author of *The Psychoanalytic Movement*, 'an almost comic contrast between the overwhelming and genuine evidence for this one phenomenon and the sketchy, dubious evidence for most other psychoanalytic ideas' (54). In the present chapter I swim against the current in making the case that all is not right with the theory of transference, and that as it stands the theory is not defensible.

The theory of transference has had a long and chequered history. Freud introduced the term, or rather its German original (*Übertragung*), in the *Studies on Hysteria* (Freud and Breuer, 1895), where it was used to denote patients' inappropriate and unwarranted displacement of ideas and memories onto their analyst. By way of illustration, Freud recounted an example of a woman who, having repressed a desire that her employer boldly give her a passionate kiss, found herself wishing that Freud would do the same. It was only after they had explored her feelings about Freud that the woman reported the previously repressed longing for a kiss from her boss.

This purely clinical conception of transference gave way to a more general psychological notion in *The Interpretation of Dreams* (Freud, 1900). Here, transference is described as a hypothetical and by definition unobservable process in which the charge of 'psychical energy' attached to a repressed idea becomes displaced onto an innocuous preconscious idea which is in some way associatively linked with it. The innocuous idea then becomes a proxy for the more emotionally explosive and potentially anxiety-provoking unconscious thought. So, for example, the repressed thought of engaging in oral sex with one's father might become expressed indirectly by the thought of enthusiastically sucking on a large red lollypop. In this example, there is what Freud (1900) called a 'transference of intensity' from an unconscious craving for one's father's penis onto the thought of eating a lollypop, as psychical energy is moved from the former to the latter, and as a result the desire for a lollypop becomes disproportionately intense. According to *The Interpretation of Dreams*, transference is the main process by means of which unconscious mental contents express themselves in consciousness and behaviour. Clinical transference, or transference onto the analyst, is just a special case of this process. The 'intensity' or emotional charge connected to an unconscious mental representation of the patient's mother or father (or, in the Kleinian system, parts of them) is displaced onto the patient's mental image of the analyst. The analyst becomes an emotional substitute for mother or father, and becomes the target of the patient's childish fantasies, fears, desires and defences. Freud, and virtually all mainstream psychoanalytic theorists, have regarded the clinical concept of transference (hereafter referred to simply as 'transference') as crucial for psychoanalytic practice. The patient, it is believed, works out his or her early issues through the medium of the relationship with the analyst. It is therefore by focusing on the bizarre and anachronistic features of that relationship, as created by the patient, that it becomes possible to access and resolve repressed infantile conflicts.

The significance of the past

The concept of transference is intimately bound up with the broader issue of the role of the past in psychoanalytic theory. The criticism of psychoanalysis as 'reductionistic' mentioned in the preceding chapter is but one face of a larger commitment to anti-naturalism most blatantly displayed by those psychotherapists who take their lead from existentialism, an increasingly widespread group that includes the 'humanistic' psychology movement. From the obscure, rambling mysticism of Heidegger to Sartre's outrageous claim that human beings have no 'essence' other than what they create for themselves, these writers propound a secular version of the denial that human beings are part of nature and subject to natural laws. Nowhere is this more apparent than in the efforts to reject psychoanalysis on the grounds that it is 'deterministic'.

Psychoanalysis is indeed deterministic in the sense that it holds that all psychological events are caused. This is not the same as claiming that human beings are not able to make choices. Of course, people do make choices. They make choices all the time. Advocates of the psychoanalytic perspective simply insist these choices are themselves caused by a whole set of values, experiences, feelings, impulses and so on which stem partially from our biological make-up and partially from our life experiences. To claim that human choices are not caused is once again to assert that human beings are like mini-Gods, standing above and beyond the natural world.

Causation operates in one direction only, following the arrow of time from past to future. A commitment to determinism thus entails a commitment to the causal role of past events. The theory of trans-ference is *par excellence* an expression of the psychoanalytic com-mitment to the idea that the past shapes the present, because it holds that human beings unconsciously and compulsively repeat conflict-laden infantile relationships with significant others.

Bearing these broad points in mind, it is clear that it might be possi-ble to undercut the theory of transference at the most fundamental level by showing that there is something fundamentally mistaken about the concept of causal determinism underpinning it. Spinelli (1994) attempts to do just this by calling into question what he takes to be two cardinal psychoanalytic propositions about the role of the past; namely that psychoanalysis adheres to a 'linear' notion of causa-tion and a view that the past is fixed and unalterable. According to Spinelli, it has 'become increasingly recognized' that human behav-iour is complex and multi-layered, and that so-called linear causality does not apply to it. 'Linear causality' is not a mainstream scientific or philosophical term. Spinelli uses it to denote the idea that 'current issues can be, in theory at least, traced back directly to past unre-solved conflicts and traumatic interludes in the client's life' (162). This definition is vague, and it is not clear what is meant by 'directly' in the definition. From the context it appears that he is referring to the idea that infantile conflicts or traumatic events are both neces-sary and sufficient causes for current psychological problem states. Although strictly speaking Spinelli's definition refers to the traceabil-ity of causal influences rather than the existence or non-existence of the causes themselves, I assume that he is actually referring to the latter.

It would appear that in speaking of 'linear' causality Spinelli has in mind a kind of simple or mono-causality (the idea that there is a one-to-one relationship between causes and effects), but this interpreta-tion of psychoanalysis would be an utter travesty. As early as 1896, Freud (1896c) was using Koch's postulates to frame a very subtle, philosophically sensitive model of causal relations that may hold between neurotic conditions in the present and pathogenic experiences in the past. Freud argued that the sexual traumas that he at the time held to lie at the roots of hysteria and form what he called its 'specific aetiology' are necessary but not sufficient causes for the condition. Furthermore, he had already introduced the principle of causal overdetermination (Freud and Breuer, 1895), which he also called the 'principle of the complication of causes' (Freud, 1901) and which refers to the idea that mental events are brought about by complex concatenations of causes.

With regard to the issue of the fixity of the past, psychoanalysis shares the view held by virtually all scientific thinkers (and indeed virtually all non-scientific thinkers) that the past is fixed and unalterable. When my wife was a small child, she was once chased down the road by a large and ferocious black cat. This event is fixed for all time: it cannot be uncreated. It cannot be changed into a different event (say, a porcupine chasing her down the road). Spinelli seems to confuse the ontological issue of the fixity of the past with the epistemological issue of the fixity of our *memories* and *interpretations* (in the non-psychoanalytic sense) of past events. Of course, we edit our memories. Sometimes we abolish them entirely. But if my wife were to repress the memory of the cat attack, this would not mean that the event had never occurred. The fact that an event is misremembered or not remembered likewise need not deprive it of causal power. I do not remember learning to walk as an infant, but my learning to walk was obviously of great causal relevance to my ability to walk now. By the same token, if I were to 'remember' learning to fly an airplane rather than drive a car, I would not by virtue of this be able to operate an airplane.

Psychoanalysis cannot reasonably be faulted for failing to appreciate the lability of memory, as this is one of the most central and persistent themes of Freudian and post-Freudian theory. The fact that our memories and interpretations of past events are alterable does not mean that they are up for grabs. According to psychoanalytic theory, the manner in which memories and interpretations are transformed are in themselves causally determined by more proximal but nonetheless still past events. Both of Spinelli's arguments therefore fail as attempts to undercut the psychoanalytic conception of the causal significance of past events.

Critique of the theory of transference

Psychoanalysts have lost sight of the fact that transference is a *theory*, not a fact. As a theory, the notion of transference is open to refutation or revision, whereas as a 'fact' (or quasi-fact) it appears to be set in stone. People undergoing psychotherapy often develop extraordinarily and often inappropriately intense relationships with their therapists. This fact is not in question. It is also not transference. Transference is the claim that this and similar interpersonal phenomena are best explained by the hypothesis that psychical energy has been displaced from unconscious representations of infantile objects onto the preconscious image of the analyst. To question the notion of transference is to challenge the theory, not the clinical facts that the theory purports to explain. Grünbaum (1993) notes that the conventional use of the concept of transference is 'loaded' with theoretical assumptions. To regard a feature of a patient's relationship with their analyst as transference 'is *predicated* on the assumption that the patient's unwholesome adult dispositions are indeed *carry-overs* or *repetitions from childhood*' (248). Grünbaum makes the point, all too often lost on psychoanalytic apologists, that simply decreeing this to be true begs the question.

If the notion of transference is to be taken seriously it must possess conditions of identity; that is, there must be criteria allowing one to coherently and systematically distinguish transference from those features of the relationship that are not transference. The American psychoanalyst Ralph Greenson attempted to do this in a presentation that lucidly encapsulated the prevailing criteria used in psychodynamic writings (Greenson, 1967). According to Greenson, transference is (a) a distinctive type of human relationship, that (b) involves the experience of wishes, feelings, drives, fantasies, defences and attitudes towards another person, that (c) 'do not befit that person and which actually apply to another' (152–3) because they belong to a past relationship rather than to a present one. For Greenson, then, there are two fundamental features of transference phenomena (note that he wrongly treats transference as a phenomenon rather than as the hypothetical cause of a phenomenon). They are *inappropriate* and *anachronistic*. In fact, Greenson states that it is the inappropriate character of transference attitudes and behaviours that marks them off as anachronistic. 'Mature' and 'realistic' attitudes that are 'in accord with the circumstances' are therefore not examples of transference.

This is fine in principle, but deeply problematic in practice. Let us first consider the issue of inappropriateness. How does an analyst reach the conclusion that an attitude is 'inappropriate'? What kind of yardstick does he or she use? On Greenson's account, an 'appropriate' attitude is one that is rationally related to the analyst's actual behaviour and bearing. If, for example, a psychoanalyst conducts themself kindly and patiently, but their patient views them as aggressively impatient, it seems clear that the patient's attitude does not 'befit' the analyst, and this, according to the standard psychoanalytic account, suggests that it 'belongs' to some person in the patient's past.

Analysts measure the relative appropriateness or inappropriateness of patients' attitudes against their own knowledge of themselves. If, for example, a patient accuses an analyst of being disgusted with her, and the analyst engages in a process of introspection and concludes that he harbours no feelings of disgust towards this particular person, the analyst can legitimately conclude that the patient's attribution was faulty, a product of transference, and most likely applicable to some significant person in the patient's past.

This approach to the problem is very common. For example, Freud reported that at a particular point in his treatment of the 'Rat Man', the patient began to heap obscene verbal abuse upon Freud and his family. At the same time he buried his head in his hands, covered his face with his arm, and then jumped up suddenly and roamed about the room. The man seemed terrified, for no apparent reason. At first the Rat Man claimed that he did this because of discomfort: he could not bear saying such things while lying down comfortably. Freud suggested that the real reason for this odd behaviour was the Rat Man's unconscious fear that he [Freud] would beat him just like his father had done in the past, an interpretation with which the patient apparently agreed. Why did Freud have confidence in this interpretation? He felt that the Rat Man's fear of him was not realistic and that it must therefore be a transference from the past. His concluding remark is quite revealing. Freud states that this interpretation would have been almost self-evident to any disinterested, that is unbiased, person.

There are two broad avenues for calling this conception into question. The first is to enquire whether it is possible to meaningfully diagnose a false attribution in a way that is consistent with the psychoanalytic theory of mind. The second is to question whether such false attributions are caused by the hypothetical mechanism of transference.

Are 'transference' attributions false?

One glaring problem with transference interpretation, as exemplified by the paradigmatic example of Freud's interpretation of the Rat

Man's behaviour, is its blatant inconsistency with the Freudian conception of the mind, which states that *all* of us are victims of self-deception and that introspection simply does not provide reliable knowledge about the more emotionally charged aspects of our inner lives. Freud was not a disinterested person: he was deeply and inextricably involved, an actor in the remarkable two-person drama unfolding in his consulting room. The Rat Man was not a disinterested person either. Perhaps Freud was indeed made angry by the Rat Man's provocative comments, but could not manage to be truthful with himself about his own feelings. Perhaps, by the same token, the Rat Man collusively fell into line with Freud's self-deception in order to please him or avoid coming into conflict with him. Although these possibilities may seem far-fetched to the advocate of psychoanalysis, I will show that they are not as implausible as they might at first seem.

The fundamental question is this: How can analysts deal with the possibility that self-serving bias leads them to assess a patient's attitudes as 'unrealistic'? If they cannot make this judgement with a reasonable degree of objectivity, it follows that they cannot distinguish between transference and non-transference with a reasonable degree of assurance.

The conventional riposte to this criticism invokes the supposedly enlightening effects of psychoanalytic training. All budding psychoanalysts are required to undergo psychoanalytic treatment, called 'training' or 'didactic' analysis, to cultivate the insightfulness and self-transparency necessary for psychoanalytic work. Ignoring the question-begging nature of this response (how can the analysts' analysts discriminate between transference and nontransference?), the history of psychoanalysis does not inspire confidence in the claim that psychoanalysts are in possession of such profound self-knowledge. Apart from its being incompatible with psychoanalytic theory, not only is there no *evidence* that analytic training is able to bring about these splendid effects, but also the whole idea 'of knowledge even, *or especially*, of oneself and one's own inner states, attained by direct contact and not dependent on theoretical or conceptual assumptions, is absurd' (Gellner, 1985: 92).

Transference as an institutionalized defence mechanism

Allegiance to the concept of transference has become a badge of membership of the psychoanalytic movement. No other psychoanalytic concept is invoked so frequently and criticized so rarely. Questioning the cogency of the transference concept elicits the kind of incredulity that would greet an assertion that the world is flat. Ernest Gellner (1985) reminds us that:

> An idea does not have simply a cognitive role, as a recipe for predictions, etc. it is at the same time linked to a set of personal relations, to loyalties, hierarchies, sentiments, hopes and fears. To shake the idea would be to disturb all that. Most men are neither willing nor able to do that. When men speak they thereby reaffirm the content of their shared concepts and their associations; they seldom and only within carefully delimited spheres, exchange information not already prejudged by the terms and context of their speech. The reaffirmation and celebration of conceptual consensus and of its value loading ... is a far more pervasive function of language than the exchange of unprejudged information. (157–8)

The concept of transference is a prime exemplar of this function. At least in its standard formulations, transference is conceptually dispensable: psychoanalysis could get along without it while still preserving its disciplinary identity, unlike, say, the concept of the unconscious which really is one of the foundations of the whole structure. Transference is important for other, non-cognitive reasons. It is emotionally necessary, because it provides a method of protecting the analyst's idealized self-image, and it is socially necessary because it allows members of the profession to collectively protect that image against the doubts that disturb it from time to time.

A few psychoanalysts have suggested that the concept of transference can be used by clinicians as a way of avoiding self-awareness (Smith, 1999d), but these critiques from within the tradition normally question the *abuse* of transference without calling into question the validity of the concept *per se*. An important step in this direction was taken by Thomas Szasz, of anti-psychiatry fame, in a paper written during the earlier part of his career when he identified himself as a psychoanalyst. Szasz (1961) states that whatever its cognitive-explanatory virtues, the notion of transference has a fundamentally self-protective function in the analytic situation. Its invocation is a way that psychoanalysts defend themselves against the unique emotional intensity of the analytic situation:

> The analytic situation is ... a paradox; it stimulates, and at the same time frustrates, the development of an intense human relationship. In a sense, analyst and patient tease one another. The analytic situation requires that each participant have strong experiences, and yet not act on them. Perhaps this is one of the reasons that not only many patients, but also many therapists, cannot stand it: they prefer

to seek encounters that are less taxing emotionally, or that offer better opportunities for discharging affective tensions in actions. (437)

How do analysts stand it? How do they tolerate being battered by patients' hatred without retaliating, being exalted by their idealizations without becoming grandiose and being the object of their sexual desires without yielding to temptation? The idea of transference provides a shield protecting the practitioner from 'too intense affective and real-life involvement with the patient' by means of a 'denial and repudiation of the patient's *experience qua experience*' (ibid.). Transference interpretations 'provide a ready-made opportunity for putting the patient at arm's length' (438).

Szasz was a reformer, not a revolutionary in his attitude towards transference. He did not question the existence of the 'phenomenon' of transference, nor did he reject the theory. The recognition of transference is described in laudatory tones as 'perhaps Freud's greatest single contribution' (438). It is an 'inspired and indispensable' concept because it allows psychoanalysts to psychologically cope with forms of emotional intensity which would otherwise be too powerful to bear while sustaining their professional role. However, it is also a dangerous concept because it allows the analyst to 'abuse' the analytic situation by placing the psychoanalyst 'beyond the reality testing of patients, colleagues and self' (443). Anything and everything can be attributed to the patient's distorted perception, and as a result the analyst is exempted from the need to take responsibility for his or her own actions. In the final analysis, Szasz concludes that the fault lies not in the concept of transference, for which he clearly has high regard, but in the moral character of those who make use of it. 'No one,' writes Szasz, 'psychoanalysts included, has discovered a method to make people behave with integrity when no one is watching' (442).

Not all analysts have been so sanguine. Some analysts, such as Merton Gill and Robert Langs, have by and large rejected the concept of transference because of its unrealistic assessment of psychoanalysts' self-knowledge on the one hand and its automatic privileging of the analyst's interpretation of the therapeutic relationship on the other. Langs (1986) has been particularly iconoclastic in this respect, remarking that during the period when he worked as a conventional psychoanalytic practitioner, clinical theory, as exemplified by the theory of transference, offered him 'considerable protection' because 'The patient was always accountable for what happened in treatment, and I was accountable only on occasion' (1).

Shlien (1984), a Rogerian therapist, takes the critique further (strangely, without citing Szasz) with the assertion that 'transference is a fiction to protect the therapist from the consequences of his own actions' (170), asserting that the so-called 'positive transference', in which the patient falls in love with the therapist, is an entirely natural product of three elements of the analytic relationship: the dependency of the patient, the patient's need for sexual companionship, and the therapist's attitude of understanding. The fact that a patient's 'transference attitude' resembles their childhood attitude toward a parent does not lead inescapably to the conclusion that it is a replay of the original relationship. Perhaps, suggests Shlien, the positive 'transference' is merely elicited by a repetition of the same general circumstance: the provision of understanding. By the same token, misunderstanding by the therapist provokes negative feelings in the patient, just as misunderstandings by parents evoke negative feelings in children. In Shlien's view, then, therapists on the whole get the responses that they deserve. The therapist 'is loved for what makes him lovable, hated for what makes him hateful, and all shades in between' (174).

Neither Szasz nor Shlien offer anything much in the way of logical or evidential support for their conclusions. Both use the example of Breuer's treatment of 'Anna O' to illustrate their thesis, a choice that is particularly unfortunate in light of the fact that historical scholarship that was unavailable to Szasz but was published over a decade before Shlien wrote his paper demonstrates the unreliability of Breuer's published account of this case (Ellenberger, 1972; Borch-Jacobsen, 1996). There is simply not enough good information on Breuer's relationship with his young patient to support claims about the nature and origins of the theory of transference. The absence of evidence undermines Shlien's claim more seriously than it does Szasz's, as the latter confines himself to the more modest proposal that the concept of transference is open to abuse. Shlien's story also begs the very question being addressed, by stating that the element of dependency in the psychoanalytic relationship sets the stage for the emergence of the phenomenon (mis)explained as transference. In psychoanalytic theory from Freud onwards, the attitude of emotional dependency is itself regarded as an expression of transference. Shlien also fails to consider the whole range of phenomena that come under the umbrella of transference, confining himself to rather global attitudes of love and hate whilst ignoring very specific fantasies that emerge in psychoanalytic treatment which appear to have a clear link with the patient's infantile past. Finally, Shlien's thesis entails the extremely implausible proposition that patients' attitudes towards their therapists are always justified by their therapists' behaviour. Although in ordinary life we are capable of bearing grudges for imaginary slights, falling in love with those who do not care for us, and fearing those who bear us no ill will, if we are to believe Shlien these unfortunate propensities promptly vanish as soon we enter the psychotherapeutic setting!

Transference at the analyst's behest?

Psychoanalytic theory understands transference as a basic human propensity rooted in the persistence of infantile desires and fears locked away in the repressed unconscious sector of the mind. The less one knows oneself, the greater one's tendency to blindly transfer. The disposition to transference is said to flower in the permissive, facilitating environment of the psychoanalytic setting. Transference is believed to be evoked by both the physical properties of the setting (such as the regularity of sessions, the analyst's reliability, the patient reclining with the analyst sitting out of sight, and its privacy and confidentiality, which protect the patient from the prying eyes and ears of third parties) and by the way that competent analysts conduct themselves. A good deal of psychoanalytic choreography is designed to foster the development of transference and ensure its analysability. Considering these facts in a more sceptical light, we might wonder whether the transference relationship is simply an *artefact* of psychoanalytic treatment. Far from being a natural phenomenon vivified by the psychoanalytic relationship, might not transference be something unwittingly created by the analyst for the analyst? Might, in short, transference be unnecessary and extrinsic to psychoanalysis?

Critics both internal and external to psychoanalysis have raised versions of this criticism. The former understand the psychoanalytic relationship as a spiralling interaction, as Langs (1980) felicitously describes it, in which the two participants co-create the phenomena that occur. One of the earliest and most lucid statements of this position was articulated by the Kleinian analyst Heinrich Racker (1958), who wrote that 'Transference is ... an unconscious creation of the analyst ... Just as countertransference is a 'creation' of the patient' (178). In 1966, Barranger and Barranger gave this position theoretical underpinnings in their paper on 'Insight in the analytic situation' in which they claimed that *everything* that happens in the analytic situation is a product of three factors: the psychoanalytic setting, the internal world of the patient, and the internal world of the analyst, thus creating a 'bi-personal field' in which the analyst shapes the patient's experience at least as much as the patient shapes the analyst's (Barranger and Barranger, 1966). This line of enquiry has been greatly extended by Harold Searles (1979) and Robert Langs (for example, 1980).

The precise implications of this approach to transference depend upon the degree to which so-called transference is causally dependent on the analytic set-up. It may well be that these phenomena are simply *cultivated* and purified by the analytic arrangement, as the majority of psychoanalysts assert. The more radical view, that the analytic situation *creates* transferences, is compatible with the claim that suggestion may play a central role in the generation of apparent confirmations of psychoanalytic theory, and has hardly been considered in the literature.

Countertransference

Although they place immense emphasis on the general human tendency to resist, repress and otherwise defend against unsavoury aspects of the inner world, psychoanalysts place little emphasis on their *own* propensity for self-deception. This state of affairs is fully consistent with psychoanalytic theory, which claims that human narcissism causes our view of ourselves to be defensively slanted in our own favour.

The issue of analysts' self-deception comes under the umbrella of 'countertransference', a term coined by Freud, but which he mentioned only four times, in just two of his works (Freud, 1910b, 1914b). Freud used the prefix 'counter' in 'countertransference' to emphasize its *reactive* character: he regarded it as a response to the patient's transference. Countertransference thus refers to analysts' difficulties *as activated by their patients' behaviour*. As Freud wrote to Jung on New Year's Eve, 1911: 'We must never let our poor neurotics drive us crazy. I believe an article on "counter-transference" is sorely needed; of course, we could not publish it, we should have to circulate copies among ourselves' (McGuire, 1974: 253).

Freud struggled to find an effective strategy for constraining countertransference. At first, he recommended continuous self-analysis (1910b), but soon concluded that analysts' emotional resistances made this impracticable. Two years later, he recommended training analysis to eliminate the unconscious conflicts held responsible for countertransference (1912b), but this also proved insufficient and in the end he urged analysts to undergo re-analysis every five years (1937). Once out, the genie could not be put back in the bottle. Freud's increasingly desperate measures suggest that there is something intractable about the problem of countertransference.

Countertransference is discussed far more extensively in the later psychoanalytic literature, but the meaning of the term underwent an extraordinary shift. Freud had occasionally argued that all individuals possess an unconscious capacity to understand the unconscious concerns of others. Beginning in the late 1940s and continuing through the 1950s, psychoanalysts began to subsume this hypothesized *cognitive* process under the rubric of countertransference, which, as we have seen, was developed by Freud to perform a very different conceptual task. Before long, the original meaning of countertransference became all but forgotten in the stampede towards the new concept. The crucial moment in this transformation was the publication of Paula Heimann's (1950) *On Countertransference*, which redefined countertransference, redeeming and exulting it beyond all recognition. In her hands, the original meaning of the term was inverted. Countertransference was now described as an expression of psychoanalysts' unconscious *sensitivity*: analysts' 'inappropriate' fantasies and emotions were said to be evoked by their *patients'* unconscious conflicts. Countertransference is therefore 'the patient's *creation*' (77) and an expression of patients' (rather than psychoanalysts') psychological problems. Heimann's approach to the problem of countertransference became wildly popular, and is now the predominant view in most regions of the psychoanalytic universe. With Heimann, countertransference came out of the closet. Analysts were now prepared to openly admit to experiencing it because what was once regarded as a psychoanalytic sin had been miraculously transfigured into a virtue. It is hardly necessary to point out that the shift had nothing to do with objective evidence. There have never been attempts to empirically assess the claim that analysts are able to make valid inferences about their patients' unconscious conflicts on the basis of the affects and fantasies that they experience during analytic sessions. Given this lack of evidence and lack of concern with evidence, analysts' widespread hospitality to the revised conception of countertransference gives the appearance of being motivated at least as much by self-serving psychological defences as by concern with psychoanalytic truth.

An obvious criticism of the Heimannian notion of countertransference is that it gives analysts *carte blanche* to misattribute their own fantasies and conflicts to their patients' unconscious minds. In fact, this very concern was raised by Melanie Klein, who was hardly an exemplar of epistemological rigour (Grosskurth, 1987). Heimann was not entirely insensitive to the charge that her approach was open to abuse, but her response was unequal to the problem: 'When the analyst in his own analysis has worked through his infantile conflicts and anxieties … so that he can easily establish contact with his own unconscious, he will not impute to his patient what belongs to himself' (ibid.). But who on earth has 'worked through his infantile anxieties and conflicts'? Who is really able to 'easily establish contact with his unconscious'? Heimann's 'safeguards' can only be maintained with a generous helping of self-deception.

Heimann inadvertently provided a magnificent example of psychoanalytic self-deception in the context of a vignette describing a patient who reported a dream in which 'He had acquired from abroad a very good second-hand car which was damaged' (1950: 76). The patient spontaneously interpreted the car as a representation of Heimann, an interpretation with which she concurred. She goes on to assert that 'The dream shows that the patient wished me to be damaged' (ibid.), a desire that allegedly sprang from his sadistic impulses. Her attitudes towards the negative and positive images in the dream are brazenly inconsistent, for she takes on board the image of herself as a 'very good' car, but unhesitatingly attributes the car's damage to the patient's unconscious wish to harm her. Why didn't Heimann infer that the patient had accurately perceived that she really was in some sense damaged? After all, according to psychoanalysis we are all in some sense damaged. The psychoanalytic rulebook would have allowed this move, but Heimann apparently did not even consider it. She seems to have been operating on the principle that analysts should treat every unflattering image of themselves as their patient's wishful distortion rather than as an accurate representation. This kind of thinking is common in psychoanalysis. It is very rare to find a psychoanalyst who is prepared to interpret an unflattering image as an accurate or even plausible representation of themselves. Heimann's interpretation of her patient's dream shows how fragile psychoanalysts' self-knowledge really is and how, in spite of self-analysis, training analysis and re-analysis, they are every bit as vulnerable to self-deception as ordinary, untrained and unanalysed folk. It is ironic that analysts' privileging of the new concept of countertransference is precisely what Freud's original notion of countertransference would lead one to expect!

Countertransference: an alternative perspective

Evolutionary psychology has a good deal to say about self-deception and provides an outlook on analysts' propensity for countertransference that is rather different from the conventional psychoanalytic story. The evolutionary theory of self-deception grew out of attempts to hammer out a biological theory of altruism. Mutual sacrifice in a co-operative social group confers immense benefits on all members of the community, but a population of pure altruists, who share indiscriminately with one another, is extremely vulnerable to exploitation. When confronted with ruthlessly self-serving individuals, the altruists become 'suckers' who are unable to defend their interests. On the other hand, entirely self-serving individuals cannot reap the rewards of mutual support and solidarity. Robert Axelrod (1984) demonstrated that the most robust interactional strategy is to co-operate with the altruists and to default on the exploiters. To do this you have to be able to distinguish the 'good guys' from the 'bad guys'. Exploitation is often covert and difficult to detect. Effective exploitation is typically a 'con': the 'mark' mistakenly thinks that they are obtaining some reward. The victim realizes all too late, if at all, that they have been taken advantage of. In other words, exploitation by means other than brute force requires the use of deception.

Deception abounds in the natural world (Otte, 1975; Wickler, 1968; Dawkins and Krebs, 1978). Consider the looking-glass orchid, *Orphys speculum*, which mimics a female wasp. The flowers of *Orphys speculum* are small, nectarless but striking in colour.

> The brilliant polished surface of the center of the flower shines like a blue-steel looking glass, edged with gold and set in a velvety maroon background. These colors are rare in the plant kingdom but are common in the kinds of wasps, bees and flies that are attracted to *Orphys*. In fact, the plant achieves a remarkable likeness to the appearance of female wasps of the species *Scolia ciliata*, the primary pollinator of *Orphys speculum*. The blue-violet center of the flower resembles the reflections from the halfway-crossed wings of a resting female. A thick set of long, red hairs imitates the hairs found on the insect's abdomen. The antennae of the female wasp are beautifully reproduced by the upper petals of the orchid which are dark and threadlike. (Trivers, 1985b: 402–403)

The orchid generates its own 'orchid pornography' to exploit the wasp's sexual instinct for its own ends. Male wasps respond by trying to copulate with the orchid.

> Male *Scolia* wasps are strongly attracted to these flowers and land on them as they would land on a female's back. The result is a pseudo-copulation: the male presses himself down on the labellum or lip of the orchid, moves about rapidly, and probes the hairy structures with his copulatory structure, apparently searching for the complementary female structure. In some species, during the male's movements he thrusts his head against the base of the pollen-bearing structures, which become attached to the male's head. In others, the male turns around and the pollen structures become attached to his abdomen. In either case, the male's search for the 'female' he has spotted leads him to carry pollen from flower to flower. (405)

The deception of the *Scolia* wasp by the *Orphys* orchid involves three steps. First, the orchid releases a strong scent that mimics the pheromones released by female wasps. This scent is so effective that male wasps often prefer the scent of the orchid to that of real females! When sexually aroused male wasps approach the source of this seductive scent they think that they have found a receptive female. At this point tactile deception takes over.

> The upper surface of the flower (the lip or labellum) has evolved a series of rigid hairs that mimic the hairy abdomen of the female insect and that males use to orient themselves during copulation. The male's movements are coordinated by the precise topography of the hairs. (ibid.)

The orchid manipulates the wasp with incredible precision.

> The labellum of the flower appears to be the main source of the sexual smell. In scratching the surface of the labellum, or in biting it (in apparent frustration), the visiting male releases further pheromones, which increases his excitement. … Yet no one has seen a male ejaculate. Instead, he seems to be caught in a world of hyperarousal that lacks the specific stimuli for provoking ejaculation. … Thus the male's interest is not diminished. Sexually intoxicated by the strong scent, the male moves about energetically in search of consummation and is unconsciously steered by the plant's hairs to pick up pollen for transfer to another flower. Failing to copulate, he flies in search of another female. (ibid.)

The wasp gets a cheap thrill but is tricked into an act that provides him with no real benefits, whereas the orchid gets to spread its genes around at no cost to itself. If we look at the interaction between wasp and orchid as a kind of exchange – sex for pollination – it is clear how the wasp has turned out to be the sucker. The wasp has been 'stung'.

There is a sizeable body of research suggesting that evolution of primate intelligence may have been driven by the adaptive advantages of social manipulation (Humphrey, 1976; Byrne and Whiten, 1988;

Whiten and Byrne, 1988; Byrne, 1993, 1994). This 'Machiavellian intelligence' hypothesis suggests that human intelligence was shaped by the need to effectively deceive our conspecifics and to second-guess their efforts to hoodwink us in the baroque choreography of deception and counter-deception that makes up the fabric of human social life. An organism equipped to deceive and exploit others possesses a potent asset in the struggle for survival. By the same token, an organism that can detect covert manipulation and take appropriate action is more likely to survive and reproduce than one that cannot. Accordingly 'as deception increases in frequency, it intensifies selection for detection, and as detection spreads, it intensifies selection on deceit' (Trivers, 1985b: 395) in a spiralling co-evolutionary arms race.

A problem with conscious deception is the deceiver's emotional response to the ever-present possibility of being discovered. Deceit is often betrayed by involuntary leakage or deception clues (Ekman, 1992). Being caught cheating can have grave or even fatal consequences, so the danger of being found out is likely to cause stress. Stress may bring about involuntary modifications of posture, changes of voice pitch and movements (Ekman, 1988, 1992), which in turn enhance the likelihood of being detected. According to Trivers (1976, 1981, 1985b, 1988), whose account of self-deception was briefly mentioned in Chapter 2, self-deception was nature's solution to this delicate problem.

> In our own species we recognize that shifty eyes, sweaty palms, and croaky voices may indicate the stress that accompanies conscious knowledge of attempted deception. By becoming unconscious of its deception, the deceiver hides these signs from the observer. He or she can lie without the nervousness that accompanies deception. (Trivers, 1985b: 415–16)

And therefore ...

> Biologists propose that the overriding function of self-deception is the more fluid deception of *others*. That is, hiding aspects of reality from the conscious mind also hides these aspects more deeply from others. An *unconscious* deceiver is not expected to show signs of the stress associated with consciously trying to perpetrate deception. (Trivers, 1988: vii)

The evolution of language significantly enhanced our capacity for self-deception.

> With the advent of language in the human lineage, the possibilities for deception and self-deception were greatly enlarged. If language

permits the communication of much more detailed and extensive information ... then it both permits and encourages the communication of much more detailed and extensive misinformation. A portion of the brain devoted to verbal functions must become specialized for the maintenance of falsehood. This will require biased perceptions, biased memory, and biased logic; and these processes are ideally kept unconscious. (Trivers, 1981: 35)

This had implications for the structure of the human mind. The falsehoods generated by the verbal module deceive the conscious mind, while true information is retained in the unconscious: 'The mind must be structured in a very complex fashion, repeatedly split into public and private portions, with complicated interactions between the subsections' (ibid.). Human beings are evolved self-deceivers (Alexander, 1975; Dawkins, 1976). Because we are reluctant to see in others what we refuse to recognize in ourselves, there is a collective denial of the role of deception and exploitation in social life (Alexander, 1975), creating 'a culture of admonitions to altruism and expectations of self-sacrifice ... with everyone having a selfish interest in the altruism of everyone else' (Badcock, 1994: 75). If the sociobiological theory is true, then psychoanalysts' attempts to defeat the power of countertransference by means of introspective self-knowledge is Quixotic. The propensity to countertransference is hard-wired into our nervous systems. It comes to us as effortlessly as breathing. It is intrinsic to human nature, and we can no more overcome it than we can overcome human nature itself.

If deception and self-deception are as pervasive as evolutionary psychologists aver, we should find evidence of this in the history of psychoanalysis. We should find that, in spite of their theoretical training and personal analysis, psychoanalysts are every bit as prone to self-deception as everyone else. This issue is the focus of Chapter 7.

7
Integrity in Focus

Psychoanalysis has always laid claim to a special relationship with the idea of truth. Freud regarded himself, and has been widely regarded by others, as a man who disturbed the sleep of the world by unmasking the hidden core of the human psyche and the unconscious, instinctual wellsprings of human behaviour. The philosopher Walter Kaufmann expressed the sentiments of many when he proclaimed that 'Freud had extraordinarily high standards of honesty' (Kaufmann, 1980: 102).

It was in this spirit that Freud's heirs set out to penetrate the veils of self-deception in order to confront and overcome the demons lurking at the heart of human nature. However, there is often a sharp contradiction between the public face of psychotherapy and the reality that lies behind it. One does not have to look far in the professional literature to find insight-orientated psychotherapists describing themselves as possessing a superior level of self-awareness and emotional maturity that is simply unavailable to the ordinary layperson. Therapists' penetrating self-insight is attributed primarily to the effect of their having undergone a rigorous training analysis, which has dissolved the sedimented layers of resistance to psychological truth. This new-found personal insight is allegedly what allows psychotherapists privileged access to the souls of others.

This grandiose neo-Cartesian idea of privileged access to the depths of one's own mind is unacceptable on a purely intellectual level. Not only is it inconsistent with the Freudian theory of mind, but also with the behaviourist views of B.F. Skinner and the research of contemporary cognitive science (Flanagan, 1991). From a less rarefied perspective, it is a sad fact that many psychotherapists are deeply troubled individuals whose lives are riven by emotional conflicts, psychological symptoms and chaotic interpersonal relationships. These realities are rarely written about. They are known only to 'insiders' (as I was for 20 years of my life) and concealed from the public gaze. In the cold, unforgiving light of reality, the lives of many of these paragons of insight make a very sad spectacle indeed.

Of course, no one should be stigmatized because they suffer from psychological problems. Freud taught us the truly liberating message that we *all* suffer from neurotic conflicts, self-deceptions and so on, and that 'normal' people are just people whom one does not know very well. However, therapists promote the idea that they are relatively free of neurotic problems. This viewpoint is enshrined in psychoanalytic language and practice. Patients transfer, whereas analysts *counter*transfer in response to the patients' craziness. Analysts sometimes suffer from '*residual* psychopathology', that minimal amount of neuroticism left over from an otherwise '*full* analysis'. In practice, analysts treat their patients' communications and behaviours as saturated with unconscious meaning, whereas analysts' interventions are regarded as possessing manifest content only. Of course, this situation extracts an emotional cost. Every practitioner knows that he or she cannot live up to these impossible ideals. I have personally known moderately famous and highly regarded psychotherapists who suffered from severe psychological problems and who felt unable to seek out professional help because they were frightened of what their colleagues might think of them. During training such problems may be dealt with by concealing them from the training analyst, so as not to be excluded from the system. Robert Langs, one of the few psychoanalysts to challenge this aspect of the professional *status quo*, remarked of his own training that 'All that a training analysis does is give you a new form of madness. ... When I finished my [training] analysis I thought "Hey, we're the elite: we've been analysed." But if anything, we are really in worse shape than anybody. We've gone in the other direction' (Smith, 1989: 119).

If high levels of self-deception are pervasive amongst the practitioners of the psychoanalytic art, we would expect to discover that this has significant ramifications for their work with suffering people. Thanks to the work of historians, the reminiscences of elderly psychoanalysts and the autobiographical accounts of victims of psychoanalysis, it is now possible take a glimpse behind the curtain. The picture is often not a reassuring one. Boundary transgressions were common amongst the early psychoanalysts. The list of analysts who had sexual relationships with their patients contains many major figures, including Georg Groddeck, Michael Balint, Carl Jung, Sandor Rado, Otto Rank, Wilhelm Reich, Rudolf Löwenstein, Marie Bonaparte, Masud Khan and Karen Horney, a list that Falzeder (1993) describes as probably only the tip of an iceberg. Reich (1967) reports that the early analysts frequently masturbated female patients under the pretence of giving them vaginal examinations. Some analysed their own children (for example, Freud, Klein, Abraham, Jung and Kris). Anna Freud analysed her own nephews. Horney and Bonaparte had their children analysed by their lovers. Still others, like Klein, had their children analysed by their own trainees. Amongst the early analysts 'the blurring of borders between professional and intimate relationships was the rule and not the exception' (Falzeder, 1993: 188). A comprehensive history of the tragic consequences of these violations, their transmission from one psychoanalytic practitioner to the next, and their impact on current psychoanalytic practice, has yet to be written.

The history of psychoanalysis is strewn with horror stories. Between 1902, when the Vienna Psychoanalytic Society was established, and 1938, when it was disbanded, at least 9 of the 149 members of the Vienna Psychoanalytic Society are known to have killed themselves (Falzeder, 1993), a fact that suggests that many of the analysts suffered from more than Freud's 'ordinary unhappiness'. Other examples, although true, are scarcely believable. I will, for want of space, concentrate on just one of them: the story of Margaret Mahler. Margaret S. Mahler is rightly regarded as an outstanding contributor to the study of infant development and childhood psychopathology. I will not concern myself with Mahler's contributions to psychoanalysis and developmental psychology. Instead, I will consider her brutal psychoanalytic treatment at the hands of her training analyst Helene Deutsch which, I will suggest, may have been a re-enactment of Freud's abusive treatment of Deutsch herself. Of course, in presenting this example I am vulnerable to the charge that I am creating a false impression by tendentiously choosing an extreme and unusual case. Although I cannot provide decisive supportive documentation (because such documentation does not exist), I assert that in the story of Mahler's treatment we merely find the abuses endemic to psychotherapy and psychoanalysis writ large (Langs, 1982b, 1985).

The story of Margaret Mahler

Margaret Mahler completed her university education in Vienna, where she obtained her medical qualification in 1923 and began to work as a medical researcher and paediatrician. It was at this point that she resolved to become a psychoanalyst. Mahler had known Sandor Ferenczi, the Hungarian psychoanalyst whom Freud called his 'Grand Vizier', during her teenage years in Budapest. Ferenczi used his considerable influence to arrange for her to obtain a training analysis with Helene Deutsch, one of the most prominent and powerful members of the Vienna Psychoanalytic Society. Having been accepted, she languished on a waiting list for a full four years before Deutsch began her treatment. Deutsch abandoned any pretence of neutrality or professionalism in the very first session. Mahler recalls her making the disparaging comment that she 'had taken me into analysis … 90 per cent because Ferenczi had asked her to do so, and only 10 per cent because I seemed to be "a nice human being"' (Stepansky, 1988: 60). Deutsch's conduct was not only degrading; it also proved to be unreliable. She cancelled sessions at the last minute at least once a week, and the analysis was further punctuated by Deutsch's lengthy holiday breaks. Deutsch simultaneously took Fanny von Hann-Kende, a friend of Mahler's, into analysis. Of course, Mahler and Hann-Kende compared notes. On one occasion, Hann-Kende asked Deutsch which of the two of them she preferred. Deutsch neither interpreted the question nor threw it back on her patient. Instead, she responded with awe-inspiring insensitivity.

> Invoking a simile from pathology, Mrs Deutsch compared the differences between our respective analyses to the difference between dissecting a liver with a rare and complicated condition and dissecting a mere 'nutmeg' liver – as though I were a nutmeg liver with only a very ordinary pathology. (ibid.)

As Hann-Kende's analysis was not disturbed by the incessant cancellations that Mahler suffered, it seemed clear that the cancellations were in some way motivated. Mahler suspected that Deutsch resented the fact that she was paying a reduced fee (Mahler could not afford the full fee and did not want her father to subsidize the analysis).

After little more than a year had gone by, Deutsch suddenly terminated the analysis on the grounds that Mahler was 'unanalysable' (that is, too extremely disturbed to benefit from psychoanalytic treatment). She did not honour her patient's confidentiality, and reported to Editha Sterba, a friend of Mahler, that she was psychotic. According to Freudian theory, psychotics are unanalysable because they are unable to form positive transferences. Deutsch apparently believed that Mahler was unable to form a positive transference onto her and was therefore inaccessible to psychoanalytic influence. Given Deutsch's behaviour, it is hardly surprising that Mahler may not have formed a positive relationship with her. Deutsch seems to have pathologised Mahler instead of taking responsibility for her own shortcomings and inappropriate behaviour.

Deutsch's verdict would normally have been the death-knell for any aspiration to become a psychoanalyst. Mahler reacted by falling into a state of depression. She discussed the situation with her friend, the charismatic and idiosyncratic psychoanalyst August Aichhorn. Aichhorn, who disliked hierarchies of any sort (including the Viennese psychoanalytic establishment), concocted a plan to take her secretly into analysis with him, in order for her to complete her analytic training. At the time she entered analysis with him, Mahler and Aichhorn were in love, and six months later they became lovers and continued their simultaneous sexual and 'analytic' relationships for two more years.

During their final psychoanalytical session Deutsch introduced the topic of Victor Tausk. The triangular relationship between Freud, Deutsch and Tausk has been the subject of a number of publications (for example, Deutsch, 1973; Eissler, 1971; Roazen, 1969, 1985; Vegh, 1997). According to Mahler, Deutsch washed her hands of all culpability by saying that even Freud could not analyse everybody, for example he had been unable to analyse Victor Tausk. This remark was emotionally loaded because the tragedy of Victor Tausk directly involved Helene Deutsch and, I will argue, may have indirectly involved Margaret Mahler.

Helene Deutsch began analysis with Sigmund Freud in 1918. However, in the autumn of 1919 one of Freud's famous ex-patients, the 'Wolf Man', returned to Vienna for more analysis. Freud abruptly terminated Deutsch's treatment and gave her hour to the Wolf Man. Deutsch suspected that Freud did this because he was bored with her, for on at least two occasions he had fallen asleep during her analytic sessions, his cigar dropping to the floor (Roazen, 1985). Deutsch became deeply depressed after the termination. The Wolf Man, who replaced Deutsch as Freud's patient 'over her objections' (Roazen, 1971: 466), did not even pay for his treatment. To make matters worse, Freud took up an annual collection for the Wolf Man, to which Deutsch had probably been asked to contribute.

Victor Tausk was a brilliant Slovakian psychiatrist who approached Freud for analysis in the spring of 1919. Freud felt threatened by Tausk, and referred him to Deutsch, who was at the time still in analysis with him. Deutsch was a psychoanalytic novice. In fact, Tausk was her very first psychoanalytic case. Humiliated by Freud's refusal to take him on, Tausk spoke incessantly to Deutsch about Freud who, in turn, would discuss her sessions with Tausk during her own analytic sessions with Freud. After three months of this. Freud laid down an ultimatum to Deutsch that she must either terminate Tausk's analysis or he would terminate her own.

> He explained to Helene that Tausk had caused interference in her own analysis, and that Tausk must have accepted her as his analyst with the intention of communicating with Freud through her. The burden was put on Tausk, not Helene. Tausk's success in fascinating her threatened the progress of her analysis with Freud. She felt Freud was acting like a demanding lover. ... To her it did not constitute a real choice but an order. With her unquestioned devotion to Freud she unhesitatingly communicated his decision to Tausk. Tausk's treatment ended immediately. (Roazen, 1985: 168–9)

Tausk fled into a love affair with a patient in the aftermath of the forced termination. Three months later he tied a curtain cord around his neck and put a bullet through his head, strangling himself as he fell. Freud showed no guilt about Tausk's suicide, and tried to inculcate the same callousness in Deutsch. Deutsch believed that Freud had simply repressed his enormous guilt (Roazen, 1985). On 24 July, not long after the suicide, Anna Freud, who was at the time in analysis with her father, informed him that 'I dreamed that the bride of Dr Tausk had rented the apartment in Bergasse 20 opposite us in order to shoot you, and each time you wanted to go near the window, she appeared there with a pistol' (Falzeder, 1993: 185). Freud interpreted this in terms of Oedipal jealousy rather than in terms of his daughter's concerns about his destructive practices. Deutsch had sacrificed her first patient in order to preserve her analysis with Freud, a sacrifice that proved to have been in vain. Only three months after the suicide (and six months after the termination) Freud announced to her that he was giving her hour to the Wolf Man.

It is at least arguable that Deutsch's behaviour towards Mahler was influenced by the emotional trauma she had suffered at Freud's hands. Although far from conclusive, the parallels are, at the very least, striking. Deutsch began analysing Mahler in October 1926 (Stepansky, 1988), at the very moment when the Wolf Man was once again seeking analysis with Freud (Gardiner, 1971). It is unimaginable that these circumstances would not have stirred up old wounds and conflicts. Freud did not take the Wolf Man back into treatment this time, and referred him to Ruth Mack Brunswick, whom Deutsch henceforth regarded as a rival for Freud's affection and who became 'chief among those she disliked' (Roazen, 1985: 464). In mentioning Tausk during their final session, Deutsch was implicitly comparing herself to Freud and identifying Mahler to the suicidal, melancholic Tausk. After the termination, Mahler fell into a deep depression just as Deutsch and Tausk had done after their forced terminations. Both Mahler and Tausk entered sexual relationships that involved the blurring of personal and professional boundaries in the aftermath of termination: Tausk had an affair with a patient and Mahler had an affair with her analyst. Mahler records (in Stepansky, 1988: 63) that around the time of her termination Deutsch had laid down an ultimatum to Hann-Kende, threatening to terminate her analysis if she did not break off her relationship with Mahler, repeating what Freud had done to her.

Freud's seduction theory

There is another kind of dishonesty that is found in psychoanalysis. Historians and critics have found that psychoanalytic accounts of treatment often contain blatant and definitely ascertainable departures from the truth, including the truth of whether or not the treatment was successful (Esterson, 1993). This tradition was established at the very inauguration of psychoanalysis. Breuer's dramatic account of his treatment of 'Anna O.' (*Studies on Hysteria* (Freud and Breuer, 1895)) culminated with the complete recovery of his young patient. However, in 1972 Henri Ellenberger published an account of the outcome of archival researches that demonstrated, beyond any shadow of a doubt, that not only had Breuer failed to cure her, but that he had her committed to a sanatorium at the termination of their therapy together with her symptoms still intact (Ellenberger, 1972). Freud certainly knew about this but never breathed a word of the truth in his publications. Scholarly studies of Freud's case studies have also revealed a raft of inconsistencies, and sometimes outright lies (Esterson, 1993). A prime example of the latter was Freud's treatment of Serge Pankejeff, otherwise known as the 'Wolf Man', whom Freud claimed to have cured of a crippling obsessional neurosis (Freud, 1918). We know from his memoirs, and from the journalist Karin Obholzer who found him in a geriatric home in 1974, that Pankejeff suffered from severe neurotic symptoms for the 60 years of his life *after* the conclusion of Freud's supposedly successful treatment of him (Gardiner, 1971; Obholzer, 1982).

The invention and abandonment of the 'seduction theory' remains one of the most sensational episodes in Freud's psychotherapeutic career. A great deal of very misleading information has been published, and continues to be published, about this clinical and theoretical fiasco, most notably by Freud himself in various retrospective accounts, and the critic Jeffrey Masson in his best-selling *The*

Assault on Truth (1984). Freud published only three papers on the seduction theory in the spring of 1896 (Freud, 1896a, 1896b, 1896c), and privately abandoned the theory in the autumn of 1897. Looking back on these years, the elderly Freud wrote that 'almost all my women patients told me that they had been seduced by their father. In the end I was driven to recognize in the end that these reports were untrue. ...' (Freud, 1933: 120). This account was accepted by generations of psychoanalysts. Much of this version of events is also accepted by Masson and others who dispute Freud's claim that the stories that his female patients told him were mere fantasies. In fact, even a cursory examination of the three 1896 papers and Freud's contemporaneous correspondence reveal that Freud's retrospective account bears little relation to the truth. Freud's patients did not routinely tell him that they had been seduced by their fathers or by anyone else. It was Freud himself who aggressively foisted this idea upon them. Although this fact is quite unambiguous and ridiculously easy to ascertain, it seems not to have been noticed prior to the 1970s, and has since been delineated by a number of scholars (for example, Cioffi, 1974, 1988; Esterson, 1993, 1998, 2001; Isräels and Schatzman, 1993; Scharnberg, 1993; Schatzman, 1992; Schimek, 1987; Smith, 1999d) whose work is often ignored by writers who, for some inexplicable reason, remain loyal to the traditional account.

Freud's papers on the seduction theory boldly stated that hysteria and other neurotic disorders are *always* caused by the repressed memory of a sexual experience occurring early in childhood and involving the stimulation of the child's genitals. According to Freud's theory, the original 'seduction' has a deferred action. At the time of its occurrence the seduction is of no great psychological consequence. However, after puberty, when the child becomes capable of sexual feelings, the memory is reactivated and charged with erotic significance. It produces severe emotional conflict and it is ultimately repressed. It is only when in this repressed state that the memory is able to generate neurotic symptoms.

The first person to smell a rat was the philosopher Frank Cioffi, who introduced his views in a 1973 radio broadcast entitled 'Was Freud a Liar?' (Cioffi, 1974). Cioffi pointed to the obvious fact, which no one seems to have noticed before, that Freud's retrospective accounts of the seduction theory were inconsistent with the original version presented in 1896. Freud clearly stated in these papers that his patients did *not* routinely report being seduced by their fathers (in fact, he did not even mention fathers as the primary culprits) and unambiguously claimed that the memories of seduction must be *unconscious* in order to produce neurotic symptoms. If Freud's patients had *told* him that they had been molested, this would have contradicted the very theory that he was promoting! Cioffi showed that a close reading of the original texts reveals that the alleged memories of seduction were actually forced by an overzealous Freud upon his patients. Ten years later, when the unexpurgated translation of Freud's correspondence with his friend Wilhelm Fliess was published, Cioffi's conclusions were amply corroborated. The psychoanalyst Jean Schimek, who undertook a careful study of the evidence, demonstrated that Freud used verbal and physical pressure on his patients, repeatedly asking them 'What did you see?' and 'What occurred to you?'.

> The patients ... seem to have produced visual scenes, often of hallucinatory intensity, accompanied with some display of affect, physical sensations, and motoric gestures. ... The reproduction of the seduction scenes may have often been a kind of minor hysterical attack, with both verbal and non-verbal expression, in a somewhat altered state of consciousness (Freud mentioned the similarities between the pressure technique and hypnosis). Freud readily admits that the occurrence, if not the main contents, of these episodes was strongly influenced by his insistent suggestions and relentless pressure. (Schimek, 1987: 943–4)

It was *Freud* who claimed that these states, which he called 'reproductions', were disguised memories of childhood sexual 'scenes'. He admits to exerting pressure – 'the strongest compulsion of the treatment' (Freud, 1896c: 304) – to induce these states in his patients. Freud also admits that his patients consistently denied having the memories that he imputed to them. Therapeutically, Freud's interventions seemed to have no positive impact. None of his patients were cured and one of them, whom Freud prematurely claimed to have cured of her hallucinations using this method, suffered a schizophrenic breakdown shortly afterwards. Freud terminated her treatment and committed her to a psychiatric hospital. It is hardly surprising that by August 1897 he was 'tormented by grave doubts' (Masson, 1984: 261) and a month later he revoked the theory.

It is clear that Freud's 1933 account of the seduction theory episode is very misleading. This might charitably be attributed to the failing memory of an old man recollecting events that had taken place almost 40 years earlier. This explanation does not hold water. Quite apart from the fact that Freud's memory seems to have been undimmed by advancing age, Cioffi's (1988) relentless investigations show that there may have been other, less acceptable, forces at play. Freud waited eight years before making public his rejection of the seduction theory (Freud, 1905a) and contradictions began to appear immediately in his story. Freud claimed in 1905 that he rejected the seduction theory because he had subsequently discovered that there are people who experience childhood 'seduction' but who remain mentally healthy, a reason that Cioffi rightly slates as both untrue and incoherent. It is untrue because Freud had already 'discovered' this prior to 1896. It is incoherent because Freud stated quite explicitly that childhood seduction only results in neurosis if the memory of it has been repressed. This 'discovery' therefore fails to provide reasonable grounds for rejecting the theory. He repeated the same story a year later (Freud, 1906), this time describing it as an 'unexpected discovery' that convinced him to change his views (Freud, 1906). 'How,' enquires Cioffi, 'could the fact that non-neurotics may also have been seduced in infancy have been an "unexpected discovery" when in one of the seduction papers themselves he went out of his way to emphasise it?' (1988: 63). Furthermore, in retracting the seduction theory, Freud (1906) asserted that the majority of the patients who formed the database for his 1896 reports had in fact *not* been seduced, which means that he had been mistaken in at least ten cases. How, enquires Cioffi, could Freud possibly have come to the conclusion that he had been mistaken?

> Let me confide my nasty suspicions ... Freud did not falsify his reconstructions. He merely withdrew from them. Why? Well, consider the alternative. Although there would have been no logical contradiction in Freud's maintaining both that the seduction theory was mistaken *and* that his own reconstructions were nevertheless sound, it would have strained their credulity excessively to ask his colleagues to believe that, *by chance* 100 percent of his clientele had been seduced in early childhood. (1988: 64)

Freud was caught between a rock and a hard place. If the theory was false, as he was now claiming, how had he come to attribute seductions to his patients in the first place? Doesn't this imply that there was something radically wrong with the *method* that led him to these conclusions? Freud chose to retain the method, and he either lied or deceived himself about what had really occurred in his psychotherapeutic sessions. Either way, he promulgated the falsehood that he had been deceived by the stories of his patients, rather than by the unreliability of his own methods. In retaining his method, Freud could go on to claim that his patients' 'memories' of seduction were actually derivatives of unconscious fantasies, but 'In endeavouring in this way to protect his developing system at its most vulnerable point he was, in effect, affirming his commitment to the same flawed analytic technique by means of which he had derived the erroneous confirmations of the ill-fated seduction theory' (Esterson, 1993: 30). If this surmise is true, then the psychoanalytic notion that unconscious fantasies underlie psychopathological symptoms, which is a mainstay of virtually all schools of psychoanalytic thought, is without substance and based entirely on the evasive need to protect an invalid investigative procedure.

This has deep implications for the reliability and validity of psychoanalytic theory and technique. In order for a discipline to grow, there must be safeguards in place to ensure that it possesses a real knowledge base, as opposed to a wishful thinking base. It is to this vital issue that we will turn in the next and final chapter of this volume.

8
The Future of an Illusion?

In his wonderful book on religion entitled *The Future of an Illusion* (Freud, 1927), Freud made an interesting distinction between true and false illusions. Freud defined illusions as things that we believe because we want to, rather than because the belief is warranted by evidence. If Paul bets $1,000 on a racehorse because the horse has his lucky number, and the horse actually comes in first, this would be an example of a true illusion. If, as is much more likely, Paul's lucky number wins him nothing at all, then his belief would be a false illusion.

In this final chapter, I would like to pose and tentatively answer the following question: is belief in psychoanalysis a true illusion or a false illusion? I confine myself to these two alternatives because, as I have demonstrated in the preceding chapters, psychoanalytic theory is not well supported by the evidence currently available: we do not have sound, objective evidence to underwrite the vast bulk of distinctively psychoanalytic propositions. This negative conclusion does not entail that we will never have such evidence. Perhaps one day we will. To say that there are presently no good evidential grounds for endorsing psychoanalysis does not mean that we know it to be false. It simply means that we do not have good reason to believe that it is a true account of human mental life. So, we are left with two alternatives. If, despite the present lack of evidence, the believers in psychoanalysis turn out to have been right all along, then the belief in psychoanalysis is a true illusion. Although this is theoretically possible, it is worth noting that given the methodological laxness of the discipline it would be *extremely surprising* if a substantial amount of psychoanalytic theorizing turned out to be an accurate portrayal of what really goes on in the depths of the mind. It seems more likely that the psychoanalytic theory will prove to be largely false and perhaps partially true.

This dismal conclusion is not inevitable. It is certainly possible for psychoanalysis to get back on the rails and secure a happier future. There are some definite recommendations that logically emerge from the analysis that I have undertaken in this volume. First, psychoanalysis needs to liberate itself from an excessively close attachment to a specific set of psychological theories. Notwithstanding its very considerable shortcomings, psychoanalysis has been the most sustained attempt to study scientifically the emotional life of human beings and its ramifications for human thought and human behaviour, but it has painted itself into a corner by identifying itself with a particular set of theories about the human mind. Real science progresses by refuting and discarding theories, but psychoanalysis clings stubbornly to them. If psychoanalysis is to have the future that it deserves, it must redefine itself in terms of its *domain.* Consider the example of physics. If physics were restricted to a particular theory or set of theories (say, Newtonian mechanics), then it would have been falsified and obliterated when twentieth century physics undermined the absolute truth of Newtonian mechanics. Of course, this was not the death of physics: it was one of its greatest triumphs. Physics was able to move on because it is defined by its domain: the study of the physical universe. If psychoanalysis was defined by its domain, then it would not matter if specific theories (such as the Oedipus complex) were shown to be mistaken. Psychoanalysis, too, could move on. But what exactly is the domain of psychoanalytic investigation? Any characterization is bound to be contentious. My own preference is to define psychoanalysis as the scientific discipline that investigates the ways that human beings unconsciously process emotionally charged information (Langs, 1992). As such, it would be an interdisciplinary nexus, just as Freud originally dreamed it to be (Kitcher, 1992), with inputs from cognitive science, evolutionary biology, neuroscience, linguistics and perhaps other well-developed disciplines, which could then bring their distinctive methodologies to bear on the special problems and phenomena under consideration. We would not devote precious resources attempting to establish the truth of time-honoured but evidentially unsupported claims, but would instead be asking new and meaningful questions about the unconscious mind and finding out ways to answer them. We would also be applying this hard-won knowledge to the task of alleviating human suffering, and the resolution of individual and social pathologies.

Second, psychoanalysis needs to restructure itself so as to consistently advance testable hypotheses, and devote serious attention and resources to methodological concerns. As it stands, there are simply no methodological checks on psychoanalytic claims. Psychoanalysts are given little training in research methodology and the philosophy of science, and are provided with little or no help in overcoming the inevitable human tendency to be led astray by the biases of their own subjectivity. As Popper stressed, it is all too easy to tendentiously select 'evidence' in support of one's beloved theory. Charles Babbage, the inventor of the Victorian prototype of the digital computer, colourfully described this as 'cooking'.

> Cooking is an art of various forms, the object of which is to give ordinary observations the appearance and character of those of the highest degree of accuracy. One of its numerous processes is to make multitudes of observations and out of these, to select those only which agree, or very nearly agree. If a hundred observations are made, the cook must be very unlucky if he cannot pick out fifteen or twenty which will do for serving up. (Broad and Wade, 1982: 30)

As we have seen, psychoanalysts' lack of concern for the rules of inductive inference has made 'cooking' a way of life. The selection of examples to prove a point is the rule rather than the exception in the psychoanalytic literature. Consider all of those compelling clinical vignettes that you may have read in the psychoanalytic journals. They are, by definition, cooked and thus largely devoid of evidential value. It often seems that psychoanalytic writers and their readers are not aware that there is something wrong with the practice of selectively reporting data to support a theoretical case. I do not mean to imply that selective or even fabricated examples should never be used, but they should be described as such and offered for exclusively illustrative rather than evidential purposes. Psychoanalysts need to realize that anecdotal 'evidence' is not evidence, and that clinical vignettes, which are a mainstay of psychoanalytic writing, have no probative value in scientific discourse.

Third, psychoanalysts need to be alert to the problem of the epistemic contamination of clinical data, and therefore be extremely cautious in their handling of such data. Rather than ignoring or dismissing the role of suggestion and inadvertent placebo effects, they should concentrate on finding ways to control them. They should also invest greater intellectual resources into experimental and epidemiological research.

Fourth, psychoanalysts need to resist the siren song of hermeneutics and other anti-scientific efforts at legitimizing their discipline. Although these alternatives can be very attractive, they are ultimately destructive to psychoanalysis because they prevent it from coming to grips with real problems and therefore prevent it from growing. To paraphrase Bertrand Russell, hermeneutics has all of the advantages of theft over honest toil or, in a more Freudian version, all of the advantages of the pleasure principle over the reality principle.

Fifth, the methodological problems haunting psychoanalysis should be addressed on an institutional level. In the world of hard science it is taken as a matter of course that knowledge advances only through collective efforts to constrain the inevitable human tendency to cheat. Cheating is just too tempting and, if left to our own devices, most of us just can't help ourselves. Science works against this tendency by imposing methodological discipline, emphazising replication and peer review procedures. In the world of psychoanalysis, there is virtually no attention paid to these matters at the institutional level. Psychoanalytic institutions do not maintain well-oiled mechanisms intended for safeguarding intellectual integrity. Standards are extremely loose, although the *rhetoric* of 'high standards' is often pervasive. There is little or no importance attached to replicability and appropriate methods of data selection, and the peer-review system is often politically contaminated and methodologically uninformed. Honesty is supposed to be secured entirely at the *individual* level through training analysis and clinical supervision. However laudable the inspiration behind these requirements, we poor mortals need more help than this. Supervision is inadequate because neither supervisor nor supervisee have credible constraints to keep them on track, and there is no evidence at all that undergoing psychoanalysis equips one to understand the human mind. As Frederick Crews perceptively notes:

> The Freudian community retains its self-respect by assuming that the author of a paper, because he has been analysed and officially trained, has acquired an objectivity and scrupulousness rarely found among the laity. But with the best will in the world, a Freudian innovator meets no methodological barrier against the temptation to misinterpret, embroider or censor his essentially secret case histories. Scientific responsibility is thus lodged precariously not in the watchdog process whereby investigators check the replicability of one another's announced results, but in individuals telling self-serving anecdotes about anonymous patients. In a community operating by such rules, metapsychological innovation comes cheaply – and is prized no less cheaply by guardians of established views. (Crews, 1986: 30)

The problem lies less in bad apples than it does in rotten barrels.

This problem is arguably much more acute in psychoanalysis than it is in other disciplines because of its very nature. By this I do not mean the inherent difficulty of investigating the complexities of the human mind. I am referring to our *emotional* attitude to psychoanalytic subject matter. Freud (1925) described how scientific innovations sometimes produce passionate and irrational emotional resistances because 'powerful human feelings are hurt by the subject matter of the theory' (221). The great sociobiologist Richard D.

Alexander has more recently described the plight of the scientist wishing to learn about deep human nature in language uncannily reminiscent of Freud's. He speaks of the 'resistance to self-understanding' that obstructs such efforts, leading 'not merely to scepticism, but to fear, resistance and even bitter and vituperative rejection'. 'In all the universe,' he remarks, 'the only topic we literally wish not to be too well understood is human behaviour ... even, it would seem, if that kind of understanding represents the only clear way to diminish the threat of self-extinction' (Alexander, 1987: 30). Psychoanalysis claims to study those processes and concerns that lie on the underside of consciousness and which human beings are driven to keep secret even from themselves. If this is true, then psychoanalytic research is intrinsically paradoxical: it goes against the grain of nature by attempting to illuminate precisely those things that all of us, by virtue of being human beings, would prefer to remain concealed. This problem is arguably as significant for understanding the failings of the advocates of psychoanalysis as it is for comprehending the motives of its foes. Its presence highlights the need for an exceptionally high level of methodological rigour in psychoanalytic research. Given the human resistance to self-understanding, any discipline setting out to plumb the depths of the mind must, in Freud's words, strive to 'arm herself with scepticism and to accept nothing new unless it has withstood the strictest examination' (1925: 213). The lack of methodological discipline, and the failure to consistently address this problem at the institutional level, has been a tragic failing of psychoanalysis.

As it stands, psychoanalytic theory must be seen as an illusion that is perhaps partly true and probably largely false, but even if in some far distant future ingenious researchers manage to prove that psychoanalytic theory is totally true (which, of course, would be logically impossible given the range of mutually contradictory theories making up contemporary psychoanalysis), its present-day advocates still do not have good reason for regarding it as such. Without sound evidence at their disposal, advocates of analysis are inevitably *believers*. They have acquired their convictions not from evidence but from *contagion*: from exposure to an idea that is so compelling that it has set up house in its host's mind (Dawkins, 1993). Psychoanalysis might be conceived as a Dawkinsian virus of the mind: a mental parasite bent on self-replication. Dawkins claims that infection by a mental virus engenders three symptoms: (1) 'The patient typically finds himself impelled by some deep, inner conviction ... that doesn't seem to owe anything to evidence or reason, but which, nevertheless, he feels as totally compelling and convincing', (2) the infected person regards their conviction as strong, despite not being based on evidence, and (3) the belief that mysteries are good things, to be enjoyed rather than resolved (ibid., 20–21). Anyone with more than a cursory knowledge of the history of psychoanalysis, or who has moved in psychoanalytic circles, is likely to hear in this description an eerily familiar ring. Dawkins's fourth symptom is also on the mark: 'The sufferer may find himself behaving intolerantly towards vectors of rival faiths ... [and] apostates ... He may also feel hostile towards other modes of thought that are potentially inimical to his faith, such as the method of scientific reason' (23). Dawkins goes on to note that viral convictions owe more to epidemiology than to evidence. Our psychoanalytic beliefs tend to replicate those of influential propagandists, training analysts or charismatic teachers rather than to be characterized by empirical demonstration or logical coherence.

Psychoanalysis is a uniquely important project, magnificent in conception if not in execution but burdened by the immense inertia of its own history. It would be tragic if this century-old fledgling were to wither and die instead of stretching its wings and taking flight as what it was originally intended to be: an interdisciplinary science of the emotional depths of the mind.

The guardians of psychoanalysis can and should get their act together. Whether or not they will choose to do so is another matter.

References

Abelson, R.P. (1963) 'Computer simulation of hot cognitions', in S. Tomkins and S. Mesick (eds) *Computer Simulation of Personality: Frontiers in Psychological Theory*. New York: Wiley.

Adams, H.E., Wright, L.W. Jr. and Lohr, B.A. (1996) 'Is homophobia associated with homosexual arousal?', *Journal of Abnormal Psychology*, 105: 440–45.

Alexander, R.D. (1975) 'The search for a general theory of behavior', *Behavioral Science*, 10: 77–100.

Alexander, R.D. (1987) *The Biology of Moral Systems*. Hawthorn, NY: Aldine de Gruyter.

Asch, S.E. (1956) 'Studies of independence and conformity: a minority of one against a unanimous majority', *Psychological Monographs*, 70 (9): whole number.

Axlerod, R. (1984) *The Evolution of Cooperation*. New York: Basic Books.

Bachrach, H.M., Galatzer-Levy, R., Skolnikoff, A. and Waldron, S.J. (1991) 'On the efficacy of psychoanalysis', *Journal of the American Psychoanalytic Association*, 39: 871–916.

Badcock, C.R. (1994) *PsychoDarwinism: The New Synthesis of Darwin and Freud*. London: HarperCollins.

Barranger, M. and Barranger, W. (1966) 'Insight in the analytic situation', in R. Litman (ed.), *Psychoanalysis in the Americas*. New York: International Universities Press.

Bettelheim, B. (1983) *Freud and Man's Soul*. New York: Alfred A. Knopf.

Bingham, R. (1980) 'Trivers in Jamaica', *Science 80*, (March/April): 56–67.

Bion, W.R. (1970) *Attention and Interpretation*. London: Tavistock Publications.

Bloom, H. (2000) *Global Brain: The Evolution of the Mass Mind from the Big Bang to the Twenty-first Century*. New York: Wiley.

Borch-Jacobsen, M. (1996) *Remembering Anna O: A Century of Mystification*. London: Routledge.

Bouveresse, J. (1995) *Wittgenstein Reads Freud: The Myth of the Unconscious*. Princeton: Princeton University Press.

Broad, W. and Wade, N. (1982) *Betrayers of the Truth: Fraud and Deceit in Science*. Oxford: Oxford University Press.

Brown, W. (1961) 'Conceptions of perceptual defence', *British Journal of Psychology*, Monograph Supplement No. 35.

Buller, D.J. (1999) 'De-Freuding evolutionary psychology' in Valerie Gray Hardcastle (ed.) *Where Biology Meets Psychology: Philosophical Essays*. Cambridge, MA: Bradford/MIT.

Byrne, R.W. (1993) 'Do larger brains mean greater intelligence?' *Behavioral and Brain Sciences*, 16 (4): 696–7.

Byrne, R.W. (1994) 'The evolution of intelligence' in P.J.B. Slater and T.R. Halliday (eds). *The Evolution of Behaviour*. Cambridge, England: Cambridge University Press.

Byrne, R.W., and Whiten, A. (1988) *Machiavellian Intelligence: Social Expertise and the Evolution of Intellect in Monkeys, Apes, and Humans.* New York, NY: Oxford University Press.

Cannon, B. (1991) *Sartre and Psychoanalysis: An Existentialist Challenge to Clinical Metatheory.* Lawrence: University Press of Kansas.

Cioffi, F. (1970) 'Freud and the idea of a pseudo-science' in F. Cioffi (ed.) (1998) *Freud and the Question of Pseudoscience.* Chicago: Open Court.

Cioffi, F. (1974) 'Was Freud a liar?', *The Listener*, 91: 172–4.

Cioffi, F. (1986) 'Did Freud rely on the Tally Argument to meet the argument from suggestibility?', *Behavioral and Brain Sciences*, 9 (2): 230–31.

Cioffi, F. (1988) '"Exegetical myth-making" in Grünbaum's indictment of Popper and exoneration of Freud' in P. Clark and C. Wright (eds), *Mind, Psychoanalysis and Science.* Oxford: Basil Blackwell.

Cioffi, F. (1998) *Freud and the Question of Pseudoscience.* Chicago: Open Court.

Clifford, J. (1996) 'Adlerian therapy' in W. Dryden (ed.) *Handbook of Individual Therapy.* London: Sage.

Crews, F. (1986) *Sceptical Engagements.* Oxford: Oxford University Press.

Crits-Christoph, P. (1992) 'The efficacy of brief dynamic psychotherapy: a meta-analysis', *American Journal of Psychiatry,* 159: 325–33.

Davidson, D. (1970) 'Mental events', in D. Davidson *Essays on Actions and Events.* Oxford: Clarendon.

Dawkins, R. (1976) *The Selfish Gene.* Oxford: Oxford University Press.

Dawkins, R. (1993) 'Viruses of the mind' in B. Dahlbom (ed.) *Dennett and His Critics.* Oxford: Blackwell.

Dawkins, R. and Krebs, J.R. (1978) 'Animal signals: information or manipulation?' in J.R. Krebs and N.B. Davies (eds), *Behavioral Ecology: An Evolutionary Approach.* Sunderland, MA: Sinauer.

Decker, H. (1977) 'Freud in Germany: Revolution and Reaction in Science, 1893–1907', *Psychological Issues [Monograph 41],* New York: International Universities Press.

van Deurzen, E. (1996) 'Existential therapy' in W. Dryden (ed.) *Handbook of Individual Therapy.* London: Sage.

van Deurzen, E. (1997) *Everyday Mysteries: Existential Dimensions of Psychotherapy.* London: Routledge.

Deutsch, H. (1973) *Confrontations with Myself.* New York: Norton.

Dixon, N. (1971) *Subliminal Perception: The Nature of a Controversy.* London: McGraw-Hill.

Dryden, W. (ed.) (1996) *Handbook of Individual Therapy.* London: Sage.

Duhem, P. (1914) *The Aim and Structure of Physical Theory,* (2nd ed.), Trans. Philip P. Wiener. Princeton: Princeton University Press, 1954.

Eagle, M.N. (1983) *Recent Development in Psychoanalysis.* Cambridge, MA: Harvard University Press.

Eagle, M.N. (1987) 'The psychoanalytic and the cognitive unconscious' in S. Stern (ed.) *Theories of the Unconscious and Theories of the Self.* Hillsdale, NJ: The Analytic Press.

Edelson, M. (1986) 'The evidential value of the psychoanalyst's clinical data', *Behavioral and Brain* Sciences, 9 (2): 232–4.

Edelson, M. (1988) *Psychoanalysis: A Theory in Crisis.* Chicago: University of Chicago Press.

Edmunds, L. (1988) 'His master's choice', *Johns Hopkins Magazine*, April: 40–49.

Eissler, K.R. (1971) *Talent and Genius: The Fictitious Case of Tausk Contra Freud*. New York: Quandrangle.

Ekman, P. (1988) 'Self-deception and detection of misinformation' in J.S. Lockard and D.L. Paulhus (eds), *Self-Deception: An Adaptive Mechanism*. Englewood Cliffs, N.J.: Prentice Hall.

Ekman, P. (1992) *Telling Lies: Clues to Deceit in the Marketplace, Politics and Marriage*. New York: Norton.

Ellenberger, H.F. (1970) *The Discovery of the Unconscious: The History and Evolution of Dynamic Psychiatry*. New York: Basic Books.

Ellenberger, H.F. (1972) 'The story of "Anna O.": a critical review with new data', *Journal of the History of the Behavioral Sciences*, 8: 267–79.

Erdelyi, M.H. (1985) *Psychoanalysis: Freud's Cognitive Psychology*. New York: Freeman.

Erwin, E. (1996) *A Final Accounting: Philosophical and Empirical Issues in Freudian Psychology*. Cambridge, MA: MIT.

Esterson, A. (1993) *Seductive Mirage: An Exploration of the Work of Sigmund Freud*. Chicago: Open Court.

Esterson, A. (1996) 'Grünbaum's tally argument', *History of the Human Sciences*, 9 (1): 43–57.

Esterson, A. (1998) 'Jeffrey Masson and Freud's seduction theory: a new fable based on old myths', *History of the Human Sciences*, 11 (1): 1–21.

Esterson, A. (2001) 'The mythologizing of psychoanalytic history: deception and self-deception in Freud's accounts of the seduction theory episode', *History of Psychiatry*, 12: 329–52.

Eysenck, H. (1952) 'The effects of psychotherapy: an evaluation', *Journal of Consulting Psychology*, 16: 319–24.

Falzeder, E.A. (1993) 'The threads of psychoanalytic filiations or psychoanalysis taking effect' in Haynal, A. and Falzeder, E.A. (eds.) (1994) *100 Years of Psychoanalysis*. Geneva: Cahiers Psychiatriques Genevois.

Fisher, S. and Greenberg, R. (1996) *Freud Scientifically Reappraised: Testing the Theories and Therapy*. Chichester: Wiley.

Flanagan, O.J. (1991) *The Science of the Mind*. Cambridge, MA: Bradford/MIT.

Flax, J. (1981) 'Psychoanalysis and the philosophy of science: critique or resistance?', *Journal of Philosophy*, 78: 561–9.

Fonagy, P. (ed.) (no date) *An Open Door Review of Outcome Studies in Psychoanalysis*. http://www.ipa.org.ipa/research/complete.htm

Frank, J. (1973) *Persuasion and Healing* (rev. ed.). Baltimore: Johns Hopkins University Press.

Freud, S. (1892) 'A case of successful treatment by hypnotism', *S.E.** 1.

Freud, S. (1896a) 'Heredity and the aetiology of the neuroses', *S.E.* 3.

Freud, S. (1896b) 'Further remarks on the neuro-psychoses of defence', *S.E.* 3.

Freud, S. (1896c) 'The aetiology of hysteria', *S.E.* 3.

Freud, S. (1900) 'The interpretation of dreams', *S.E.* 4 and 5.

Freud, S. (1901) 'The psychopathology of everyday life', *S.E.* 6.

Standard Edition of the Complete Psychological Works of Sigmund Freud. Trans. J. Strachey et al. London: Hogarth Press, 1953–1974.

Freud, S. (1904) 'Freud's psychoanalytic procedure', *S.E.* 7.

Freud, S. (1905a) 'Fragment of an analysis of a case of hysteria', *S.E.* 7.

Freud, S. (1905b) 'Jokes and their relation to the unconscious', *S.E.* 8.

Freud, S. (1906) 'My views on the part played by sexuality in the aetiology of the neuroses', *S.E.* 7.

Freud, S. (1909a) 'Analysis of a phobia in a five year old boy', *S.E.* 10.

Freud, S. (1909b) 'Notes upon a case of obsessional neurosis', *S.E.* 10.

Freud, S. (1910a) 'Five lectures on psycho-analysis', *S.E.* 11.

Freud, S. (1910b) 'The future prospects of psycho-analytic therapy', *S.E.* 11.

Freud, S. (1911) 'Psycho-analytic notes on an autobiographical account of a case of paranoia (dementia paranoides)', *S.E.* 12.

Freud, S. (1912a) 'A note on the unconscious in psycho-analysis', *S.E.* 12.

Freud, S. (1912b) 'Recommendations to physicians practising psycho-analysis', *S.E.* 12.

FFreud, S. (1913) 'The claims of psycho-analysis to scientific interest' *S.E.* 13.

Freud, S. (1914a) 'On narcissism: an introduction', *S.E.* 14.

Freud, S. (1914b) 'On the history of the psycho-analytic movement', *S.E.* 14.

Freud, S. (1915a) 'A case of paranoia running counter to the psycho-analytic theory of the disease', *S.E.* 14.

Freud, S. (1915b) 'Repression', *S.E.* 14.

Freud, S. (1915c) 'The unconscious', *S.E.* 14.

Freud, S. (1916–17) 'Introductory lectures on psycho-analysis', *S.E.* 15 and 16.

Freud, S. (1918) 'From the history of an infantile neurosis', *S.E.* 17.

Freud, S. (1920) 'A note on the pre-history of the technique of analysis', *S.E.* 18.

Freud, S. (1923a) 'The ego and the id', *S.E.* 19.

Freud, S. (1923b) 'Remarks on the theory and practice of dream interpretation', *S.E.* 19.

Freud, S. (1925) 'Resistances to psycho-analysis', *S.E.* 19.

Freud, S. (1926) 'Inhibitions, symptoms and anxiety', *S.E.* 20.

Freud, S. (1927) 'The future of an illusion', *S.E.* 21.

Freud, S. (1933) 'New introductory lectures on psychoanalysis', *S.E.* 22.

Freud, S. (1937) 'Constructions in analysis', *S.E.* 23.

Freud, S. (1940) 'An outline of psycho-analysis', *S.E.* 23.

Freud, S. (1950) 'Project for a scientific psychology', *S.E.* 1.

Freud, S. and Breuer, J. (1895) 'Studies on hysteria', S.E. 2.

Frosch, S. (1997) *For and Against Psychoanalysis.* London: Routledge.

Gardiner, M.M. (1971) *The Wolf Man and Sigmund Freud.* New York: Basic Books.

Gardner, S. (1993) *Irrationality and the Philosophy of Psychoanalysis.* New York: Cambridge University Press.

Gellner, E. (1985) *The Psychoanalytic Movement or the cunning of unreason.* London: Paladin.

Glymour, C. (1983) 'The theory of your dreams' in R.S. Cohen and L. Laudan (1983) *Physics, Philosophy and Psychoanalysis: Essays in Honor of Adolf Grünbaum.* Boston: Reidel.

Glymour, C. (1993) 'How Freud left science', In J. Earman, A.I. Janis and G.J. Massey (eds) (1993) *Philosophical Problems of the Internal and External Worlds: Essays on the Philosophy of Adolf Grünbaum.* Pittsburgh: University of Pittsburgh Press.

Greenson, R. (1967) *The Technique and Practice of Psycho-Analysis.* London: Hogarth.

Grosskurth, P. (1987) *Melanie Klein: Her World and Work.* Cambridge, MA: Harvard University Press.

Grünbaum, A. (1984) *The Foundations of Psychoanalysis: A Philosophical Critique*. Berkeley, CA: University of California Press.

Grünbaum, A. (1993) *Validation in the Clinical Theory of Psychoanalysis: A Study in the Philosophy of Psychoanalysis*. Madison, CT: International Universities Press.

Grünbaum, A. (1997) 'One hundred years of psychoanalytic theory and therapy: retrospect and prospect' in M. Carrier and P. Machamer (eds) *Mindscapes: Philosophy, Science and the Mind*. Pittsburgh: University of Pittsburgh Press.

Habermas, J. (1971) *Knowledge and Human Interests*. Trans. J.J. Shapiro. Boston: Beacon Press.

Hadamard, J. (1949) *The Psychology of Invention in the Mathematical Field*. Princeton, NJ: Princeton University Press.

Hamilton, W.D. (1964) 'The genetical theory of social behavior, I and II', *Journal of Theoretical Biology*, 7: 1–16, 17–32.

Haskell, R.E. (1999) *Between the Lines: Unconscious Meaning in Everyday Conversation*. New York: Plenum.

Haskell, R.E. (2001) *Deep Listening: Uncovering Hidden Meaning in Conversation*. Cambridge, MA: Perseus.

Hayek, F.A. (1978) *Three Sources of Human Values*. London: London School of Economics and Political Science.

Heimann, P. (1950) 'On countertransference', *International Journal of Psycho-Analysis*, 31: 81–4.

Hobson, J. Allan (1988) *The Dreaming Brain*. New York: Basic Books.

Holender, D. (1986) 'Semantic activation without conscious identification in dichotic listening, parafoveal vision and visual masking: a survey and appraisal', *Behavioral and Brain Sciences*, 9: 1–66.

Horgan, J. (1999) *The Undiscovered Mind*. London: Weidenfeld and Nicolson.

Hume, D. (1748) *Enquiry Concerning Human Understanding*. Oxford: Oxford University Press, 1999.

Humphrey, N. (1976) 'The social function of intellect' in P.P.G. Bateson and R.A. Hinde (eds), *Growing Points in Ethology*. Cambridge: Cambridge University Press.

Isräels, H. and Schatzman, M. (1993) 'The seduction theory', *History of Psychiatry*, 4: 23–59.

Jung, C.G. (1963) *Memories, Dreams, Reflections*. Trans. R. and C. Winston. London: Collins and Routledge & Kegan Paul.

Kandel, E.R. (1998) 'A new intellectual framework for psychiatry', *American Journal of Psychiatry*, 15: 457–69.

Kaufmann, W. (1980) *Freud, Adler and Jung: Discovering the Mind, Vol. 3*. Brunswick, NJ: Transaction.

Kernberg, O. (1994) 'Validation in the clinical process', *International Journal of Psycho-Analysis*, 75: 1193–1200.

Kihlstrom, J. (1987) 'The cognitive unconscious', *Science*, 237: 1445–52.

Kitcher, P. (1992) *Freud's Dream: A Complete Interdisciplinary Science of Mind*. Cambridge, MA: Bradford/MIT.

Klein, G.S. (1976) *Psychoanalytic Theory: An Exploration of Essentials*. New York: International Universities Press.

Kline, P. (1981) *Fact and Fantasy in Freudian Therapy*. London: Methuen.

Kline, P. (1992) 'Problems of methodology in studies of psychotherapy' in D. Dryden and C. Feltham (eds), *Psychotherapy and its Discontents*. Buckingham: Open University Press.

Kohut, H. (1959) 'Introspection, empathy and psychoanalysis', *Journal of the American Psychoanalytic Association,* 7: 459–83.

Lakatos, I. (1976) *Proofs and Refutations: The Logic of Mathematical Discovery.* Cambridge: Cambridge University Press.

Langs, R.J. (1980) *Interactions: The Realm of Transference and Countertransference.* New York: Jason Aronson.

Langs, R.J. (1982a) *Psychotherapy: A Basic Text.* New York: Jason Aronson.

Langs, R.J. (1982b) *The Psychotherapeutic Conspiracy.* New York: Jason Aronson.

Langs, R.J. (1985) *Madness and Cure.* Lake Worth, FL: Gardner.

Langs, R.J. (1986) 'On becoming a communicative analyst', published in Italian as 'Diventare uno psicoanalista communicativo', *Psicoterapia e Scienze Umane,* 3: 273–7.

Langs, R.J. (1992) *Science, Systems and Psychoanalysis.* London: Karnac.

Langs, R.J. (1996) *The Evolution of the Emotion-Processing Mind.* London: Karnac.

Lashley, K.D. (1950) 'In search of the engram', *Symposia for the Society of Experimental Biology,* 4: 454–82.

Lazar, S.G. (ed.) (1997) *Extended Dynamic Psychotherapy: Making the Case in an Era of Managed Care.* Hillsdale, NJ: The Analytic Press.

LeDoux, J.E. (1996) *The Emotional Brain.* New York: Simon & Schuster.

Libet, B. (1985) 'Unconscious cerebral initiative and the role of conscious will in voluntary action' *Behavioral and Brain Sciences,* 8: 529–66.

Libet, B. Alberts, W.W., Wright, E.W. Jr., Feinstein, B. and Pearl, B. (1979) 'Subjective referral of the timing for a conscious sensory experience', *Brain,* 102: 193–224.

Luborsky, L., Mellon, J., Alexanser, K., van Ravenswaay, P., Chidress, A., Levine, F.J., Frits-Christof, D., Cohen, K.D., Hold, A.V. and Ming, S. (1985) 'A verification of Freud's grandest clinical hypothesis: the transference', *Clinical Psychology Revue,* 5: 231–46.

MacKinnon, D.W. and Dukes, W.F. (1964) 'Repression' in L. Postman (ed.) *Psychology in the Making.* New York: Knopf.

Marmor, J. (1962) 'Psychoanalytic therapy as an educational process' in J. Masserman (ed.), *Psychoanalytic Education.* New York: Grune and Stratton.

Marr, D. (1982) *Vision.* San Franscisco: W.H. Freeman & Co.

Masson, J.M. (1984) *The Assault on Truth: Freud's Suppression of the Seduction Theory.* New York: Farrar, Straus & Giroux.

Masson, J.M. (ed.) (1985) *The Complete Letters of Sigmund Freud to Wilhelm Fliess.* Trans. J.M. Masson. Cambridge, MA: Harvard University Press.

McGuire, W. (1974) *The Freud/Jung Letters.* Trans. R. Manheim and R.F.C. Hull. London: The Hogarth Press and Routledge & Kegan Paul.

Medawar, P. (1982) *Pluto's Republic.* Oxford: Oxford University Press.

Meehl, P. (1991a) 'Some methodological reflections on the difficulties of psychoanalytic research'. *Selected Philosophical and Methodological Papers.* Minneapolis: University of Minnesota Press, 1991.

Meehl, P. (1991b) 'Subjectivity in psychoanalytic inference: the nagging persistence of Fliess' Achensee question'. *Selected Philosophical and Methodological Papers.* Minneapolis: University of Minnesota Press, 1991.

Nagel, E. (1959) 'Methodological issues in psychoanalytic theory' in S. Hook (ed.), *Psychoanalysis, Scientific Method and Philosophy.* London: Transaction Publishers.

Nesse, R.M. and Lloyd, A.T. (1992) 'The Evolution of Psychodynamic Mechanisms' in J.H. Barkow, L. Cosmides and J. Tooby (eds), *The Adapted Mind* (601–624). New York: Oxford University Press.

Nunberg, H. and Federn, E. (eds) (1962–1975) *Minutes of the Vienna Psychoanalytic Society*. Trans. H. Nunberg. New York: International Universities Press.

Obholzer, K. (1982) *The Wolf Man Sixty Years Later: Conversations with Freud's Controversial Patient*. Trans. M. Shaw. London: Routledge.

Otte, D. (1975) 'On the role of intraspecific deception', *American Naturalist*, 109: 239–42.

Panksepp, J. (2000) 'The neuro-evolutionary cusp between emotions and cognitions: implications for understanding consciousness and the emergence of a unified mind science', *Consciousness and Emotion*, 1 (1): 15–54.

Poincaré, H. (1913) *Last Essays*. Trans. J. W. Bolduc. New York: Dover, 1963.

Popper, K. (1963) *Conjectures and Refutations*. New York: Basic Books.

Popper, K. (1976) *Unended Quest*. New York: Fontana.

Rachman, S.J. and Wilson, G.T. (1980) *The Effects of Psychological Therapy*. London: Pergamon.

Racker, H. (1958) 'Countertransference and interpretation', *Journal of the American Psychoanalytic Association*, 6: 215–21.

Reich, W. (1967) *Reich Speaks of Freud*. London: Souvenir Press.

Richards, B. (1989) *Images of Freud: Cultural Responses to Psychoanalysis*. London: Dent.

Ritvo, L.B. (1990) *Darwin's Influence on Freud: A Tale of Two Sciences*. New Haven: Yale University Press.

Roazen, P. (1969) *Brother Animal: The Story of Freud and Tausk*. New York: Knopf.

Roazen, P. (1971) *Freud and his Followers*. New York: Alfred A. Knopf.

Roazen, P. (1985) *Helene Deutsch: A Psychoanalyst's Life*. New York: Doubleday.

Roth, A. and Fonagy, P. (1996) *What Works for Whom? A Critical Review of Psychotherapy Research*. New York: Guilford Press.

Sacks, O.W. (1998) 'Sigmund Freud: the other road' in G. Guttman and I. Scholtz-Strasser (eds), *Freud and the Neurosciences: From Brain Research to the Unconscious*. Vienna: Verlag der Österreichischen Akademie der Wissenschaften.

Saks, E.R. (1999) *Interpreting Interpretation: The Limits of Hermeneutic Psychoanalysis*. New Haven, CT: Yale University Press.

Sand, R. (1993) 'On a contribution to a future scientific study of dream interpretation' in J. Earman, A.I. Janis and G.J. Massey (eds), *Philosophical Problems of the Internal and External Worlds: Essays on the Philosophy of Adolf Grünbaum*. Pittsburgh: University of Pittsburgh Press.

Sandler, J. and Sandler, A.-M. (1994) 'Comments on the conceptualisation of clinical facts in psychoanalysis', *International Journal of Psycho-Analysis*, 75: 995–1010.

Sartre, J-P. (1956) *Being and Nothingness: An Essay on Phenomenological Ontology*. Trans. H. Barnes. New York: New York Philosophical Library.

Schafer, R. (1968) *Aspects of Internalization*. New York: International Universities Press.

Schafer, R. (1976) *A New Language for Psychoanalysis*. New Haven, CT: Yale University Press.

Scharnberg, M. (1993) *The Non-Authentic Nature of Freud's Observations*. 2 Vols. Stockholm: Almqvist and Wiskell International.

Schatzman, M. (1992) 'Freud: Who seduced whom?', *New Scientist,* March 21, 1999: 34–7.

Schimek, J.G. (1987) 'Fact and fantasy in the seduction theory: a historical review', *Journal of the American Psychoanalytical Association,* 35: 937–65.

Schwartz, J. (1996) 'Physics, philosophy, psychoanalysis and ideology: on engaging with Adolf Grünbaum', *Psychoanalytic Dialogues,* 6 (4): 503–513.

Schwartz, J. (1999) *Cassandra's Daughter.* London: Viking.

Searles, H.F. (1979) *Countertransference and Related Subjects.* New York: International Universities Press.

Shevrin, H. (1992) 'The Freudian unconscious and the cognitive unconscious: identical or fraternal twins' in J.B. Barron, M.N. Eagle and D.L. Wolitzky (eds), *Interface of Psychoanalysis and Psychology.* Wahington, D.C.: American Psychological Association.

Shlien, J.M. (1984) 'A countertheory of countertransference' in R.H. Levant and J.M. Shlien (eds), *Client-Centered Therapy and the Person-Centered Approach.* New York: Praeger.

Slavin, M.O. and Kriegman, D. (1992) *The Adaptive Design of the Human Psyche: Psychoanalysis, Evolutionary Biology and the Therapeutic Process.* New York: Guilford.

Smith, D.L. (1989) 'Interview with Robert Langs', *Changes,* 5 (4): 407–411.

Smith, D.L. (1994) 'Riding shotgun for Freud: a reply to Ernesto Spinelli', *Journal of the Society for Existential Analysis,* 5: 142–6.

Smith, D.L. (1995)'"It sounds like an excellent idea!": episode four of a psychological cliff-hanger', *Journal of the Society for Existential Analysis,* 6 (1): 149–60.

Smith, D.L. (1996) 'Psychodynamic therapy: the Freudian approach' in W. Dryden (ed.), *Handbook of Individual Therapy.* London: Sage.

Smith, D.L. (1999a) *Freud's Philosophy of the Unconscious.* Boston: Kluwer.

Smith, D.L. (1999b) *Approaching Psychoanalysis: An Introductory Course.* London: Karnac.

Smith, D.L. (1999c) 'Getting our act together: lessons on meaningful psychotherapy research from the philosophy of science', *Journal of Clinical Psychology,* 55 (12): 1495–1506.

Smith, D.L. (1999d) *Hidden Conversations: An Introduction to Communicative Psychoanalysis.* 2nd ed. London: Rebus.

Smith, D.L. (2000) 'Freudian science of consciousness: then and now', *Neuropsychoanalysis,* 2 (1): 38–45.

Solms, M. and Saling, M. (1986) 'On psychoanalysis and neuroscience: Freud's attitude to the localizationist tradition', *International Journal of Psycho-Analysis,* 67: 397.

Spence, D. (1982) *Narrative Truth and Historical Truth.* New York: Norton.

Spence, D. (1987) *The Freudian Metaphor: Towards Paradigm Change in Psychoanalysis.* New York: Norton.

Spinelli, E. (1993) 'The unconscious: an idea whose time has gone?', *Journal of the Society for Existential Analysis,* 4: 19–47.

Spinelli, E. (1994) *Demystifying Therapy.* London: Constable.

Steele, R.S. (1979) 'Psychoanalysis and hermeneutics', *International Revue of Psychoanalysis,* 6: 389–411.

Stekel, W. (1943) *The Interpretation of Dreams: New Developments and Technique.* Trans. E. and C. Paul. New York: Grosset and Dunlap, 1962.

Stepansky, P.E. (1988) *The Memoires of Margaret S. Mahler*. New York: The Free Press.

Stiles, W.B. and Shapiro, D.A. (1994) 'Disabuse of the drug metaphor: psychotherapy outcome-process correlations', *Journal of Consulting and Clinical Psychology*, 62: 942–8.

Strawson, P.F. (1974) *Freedom and Resentment and Other Essays*. London: Methuen.

Strenger, C. (1991) *Between Hermeneutics and Science: An Essay on the Epistemology of Psychoanalysis*. Madison, CT: International Universities Press.

Symons, D. (1987) 'If we're all Darwinians, what's the fuss about?', in C. Crawford, M. Smith and D. Krebs (eds), *Sociobiology and Psychology: Ideas, Issues, and Applications* (pp. 121–146). Hillsdale, NJ: Lawrence Erlbaum.

Szasz, T. (1961) 'The concept of transference', *International Journal of Psycho-Analysis*, 44: 432–43.

Taylor, C. (1979) 'Interpretation and the sciences of man' in P. Rabinow and W. Sullivan (eds), *Interpretive Social Science: A Reader*. Berkeley: University of California Press.

Taylor, C. (1985) 'Peaceful coexistence in psychology', in C. Taylor (ed.) *Philosophical Papers*. Cambridge: Cambridge University Press.

Thompson, J.B. (1996) 'Hermeneutics' in *The Social Science Encyclopaedia*. 2nd ed. A. and J. Kuper (eds). New York: Routledge.

Thorne, B. (1996) 'Person-centred therapy' in W. Dryden (ed.), *Handbook of Individual Therapy*. London: Sage.

Trivers, R. (1976) Foreword to *The Selfish Gene*. Oxford: Oxford University Press.

Trivers, R. (1981) 'Sociobiology and politics' in E. White (ed.), *Sociobiology and Human Politics*. Lexington, MA: Lexington Books.

Trivers, R. (1985a) Interview. *Omni*. July 1985: 77–111.

Trivers, R. (1985b) *Social Evolution*. Menlo Park, CA: Benjamin Cummings.

Trivers, R. (1988) 'Introduction' in J.S. Lockard and D.L. Paulhus (eds), *Self-Deception: An Adaptive Mechanism?* Englewood Cliffs, NJ: Prentice Hall.

Tuckett, D. (1994) 'The conceptualisation and communication of clinical facts in psychoanalysis: foreword', *International Journal of Psycho-Analysis*, 75: 865–90.

Vegh, I. (1997) *Brother Animal: one book, one story, one logic*, in T. Dufresne (ed.), *Freud Under Analysis: History, Theory, Practice*. Northvale, NJ: The Analytic Press.

Viderman, S. (1979) 'The analytic space: meaning and problems', *The Psychoanalytic Quarterly*, 48: 257–301.

Whiten, A. and Byrne, R.W. (1988) 'Tactical deception in primates', *Behavioral and Brain Sciences*, 11: 233–73.

Wickler, W. (1968) *Mimicry in Plants and Animals*. New York: McGraw-Hill.

Wilson, E.O. (1975) *Sociobiology: The New Synthesis*. Cambridge, MA: Harvard University Press.

Wittgenstein, L. (1966) *Lectures and Conversations on Aesthetics, Psychology and Religious Belief*. Berkeley, CA: University of California Press.

Wittgenstein, L. (1976) 'Ursache und Wirkung: Intuitive Erfassen' *Philosophia*. 6: 402.

Wittgenstein, L. (1982) 'Conversations on Freud: excerpt from the 1932–33 lectures' in R. Wollheim and J. Hopkins (eds.) *Philosophical Essays on Freud*. Cambridge: Cambridge University Press.

Index

Taylor, C., 74–5
thematic affinity, 102–3
theoretical entities, *see* unobservable
  entities
Thompson, J., 65
Throne, B., 3
Tooby, J., 57
topographical model, 86–7
training analysis, 115, 120, 127,
  128, 141
transactional analysis, 1
transference, 30–1, 33–4, 44, 69,
  106, 109–20, 128, 130
Trivers, R., 57–8, 59–60, 123–6
truth, 76–7, 78, 79–80
Tuckett, D., 25

unconscious, 2, 51–60, 74, 82–97,
  125–6, 135, 139
unconscious consciousness, 93–4
unconscious motives, 70
unobservable entities, 84–5

validity, 61–2
verification of theories, 11–46
Viderman, S., 76
Vienna Psychoanalytic Society,
  129, 130
viruses of the mind, 142–3

war neurosis, 25–6
Watson, J.B., 2
Whewell, W., 27
Whiten, A., 124–5
Wickler, W., 123
Williams, G., 56
Wilson, A., 61
Wilson, E.O., 56–7
Wittgenstein, L., 68–70, 73, 87,
  101, 103, 107
Wolf Man, 131, 132
Wundt, W., 2